635 PERL, Philip
PER Miniatures and bonsai

S ✓

DATE DUE

29783

STOCKTON
Township Public Library
Stockton, IL

Books may be drawn for two weeks and renewed once.

A fine of five cents a library day shall be paid for each book kept overtime.

Borrower's card must be presented whenever a book is taken. If card is lost a new one will be given for payment of 25 cents.

Each borrower must pay for damage to books.

KEEP YOUR CARD IN THIS POCKET

DEMCO

Miniatures and Bonsai

TIME
LIFE
BOOKS
®

Other Publications:

PLANET EARTH

COLLECTOR'S LIBRARY OF THE CIVIL WAR

LIBRARY OF HEALTH

CLASSICS OF THE OLD WEST

THE EPIC OF FLIGHT

THE GOOD COOK

THE SEAFARERS

THE ENCYCLOPEDIA OF COLLECTIBLES

THE GREAT CITIES

WORLD WAR II

HOME REPAIR AND IMPROVEMENT

THE WORLD'S WILD PLACES

THE TIME-LIFE LIBRARY OF BOATING

HUMAN BEHAVIOR

THE ART OF SEWING

THE OLD WEST

THE EMERGENCE OF MAN

THE AMERICAN WILDERNESS

LIFE LIBRARY OF PHOTOGRAPHY

THIS FABULOUS CENTURY

FOODS OF THE WORLD

TIME-LIFE LIBRARY OF AMERICA

TIME-LIFE LIBRARY OF ART

GREAT AGES OF MAN

LIFE SCIENCE LIBRARY

THE LIFE HISTORY OF THE UNITED STATES

TIME READING PROGRAM

LIFE NATURE LIBRARY

LIFE WORLD LIBRARY

FAMILY LIBRARY:
    HOW THINGS WORK IN YOUR HOME
    THE TIME-LIFE BOOK OF THE FAMILY CAR
    THE TIME-LIFE FAMILY LEGAL GUIDE
    THE TIME-LIFE BOOK OF FAMILY FINANCE

This volume is one of a series that offers information on the cultivation of indoor and outdoor plants and explains the principles of garden design.

Miniatures and Bonsai

by
PHILIP PERL
and
the Editors of TIME-LIFE BOOKS

TIME-LIFE BOOKS, ALEXANDRIA, VIRGINIA

Time-Life Books Inc.
is a wholly owned subsidiary of
TIME INCORPORATED

FOUNDER: Henry R. Luce 1898-1967

Editor-in-Chief: Henry Anatole Grunwald
President: J. Richard Munro
Chairman of the Board: Ralph P. Davidson
Executive Vice President: Clifford J. Grum
Chairman, Executive Committee: James R. Shepley
Editorial Director: Ralph Graves
Group Vice President, Books: Joan D. Manley
Vice Chairman: Arthur Temple

TIME-LIFE BOOKS INC.
MANAGING EDITOR: Jerry Korn
Text Director: George Constable
Board of Editors: Dale M. Brown, George G. Daniels,
Thomas H. Flaherty Jr., Martin Mann, Philip W. Payne,
Gerry Schremp, Gerald Simons, Kit van Tulleken
Planning Director: Edward Brash
Art Director: Tom Suzuki
    Assistant: Arnold C. Holeywell
Director of Administration: David L. Harrison
Director of Operations: Gennaro C. Esposito
Director of Research: Carolyn L. Sackett
    Assistant: Phyllis K. Wise
Director of Photography: Dolores A. Littles

CHAIRMAN: John D. McSweeney
President: Carl G. Jaeger
Executive Vice Presidents: John Steven Maxwell,
David J. Walsh
Vice Presidents: George Artandi, Stephen L. Bair,
Peter G. Barnes, Nicholas Benton, John L. Canova,
Beatrice T. Dobie, Carol Flaumenhaft, James L. Mercer,
Herbert Sorkin, Paul R. Stewart

THE TIME-LIFE ENCYCLOPEDIA OF GARDENING
EDITOR: Robert M. Jones
EDITORIAL STAFF FOR MINIATURES AND BONSAI:
Assistant Editor: Sarah Bennett Brash
Text Editors: Bobbie Conlan-Moore, Margaret Fogarty,
Bonnie Bohling Kreitler
Picture Editor: Neil Kagan
Designer: Albert Sherman
Staff Writers: Susan Perry, Reiko Uyeshima
Researchers: Margaret W. Dawson, Marilyn Murphy,
Clarissa Myrick, Betty Hughes Weatherley
Copy Coordinator: Elizabeth Graham
Art Assistant: Santi José Acosta
Picture Coordinator: Barbara S. Simon
Editorial Assistant: Maria Zacharias
Special Contributors: Oliver E. Allen, Margaret Carter,
Betsy Kent, Michael McTwigan, Rona Mendelsohn,
Jane Opper, Maggie Oster (text)

EDITORIAL OPERATIONS
Production Director: Feliciano Madrid
    Assistants: Peter A. Inchauteguiz, Karen A. Meyerson
Copy Processing: Gordon E. Buck
Quality Control Director: Robert L. Young
    Assistant: James J. Cox
    Associates: Daniel J. McSweeney, Michael G. Wight
Art Coordinator: Anne B. Landry
Copy Room Director: Susan B. Galloway
    Assistants: Celia Beattie, Ricki Tarlow

CORRESPONDENTS: Elisabeth Kraemer (Bonn); Margot
Hapgood, Dorothy Bacon (London); Susan Jonas, Lucy T.
Voulgaris (New York); Maria Vincenza Aloisi, Josephine du
Brusle (Paris); Ann Natanson (Rome). Valuable assistance
was also provided by: Janny Hovinga (Amsterdam); Diane
Asselin (Los Angeles); Carolyn T. Chubet, Miriam Hsia (New
York); Carol Barnard (Seattle); Yasuko Kawaguchi (Tokyo).

THE AUTHOR: The late Philip Perl wrote two other volumes, *Ferns* and *Cacti and Succulents,* for The TIME-LIFE Encyclopedia of Gardening. He was on the staff of *The New Yorker* for 20 years. In writing about plants, Mr. Perl drew on his experience as a garden designer and interior landscaper. He divided his time between Manhattan and his New Jersey blueberry farm.

CONSULTANTS: The late James Underwood Crockett, author of 13 of the volumes in the Encyclopedia, co-author of two additional volumes and consultant on other books in the series, was a lover of the earth and its good things. He graduated from the Stockbridge School of Agriculture at the University of Massachusetts and worked all his life in horticulture. A perennial contributor to gardening magazines, he also wrote a monthly bulletin, "Flowery Talks," distributed through retail florists. His television program, *Crockett's Victory Garden,* shown all over the United States, won countless converts to his approach to growing things. Dr. Robert L. Baker was Associate Professor of Horticulture at the University of Maryland, College Park. Dr. James W. Boodley is Professor of Floriculture at Cornell University, Ithaca, New York. Dr. Miklos Faust is Chief of the Fruit Laboratory at the U.S. Department of Agriculture's Agricultural Research Center, Beltsville, Md. Dr. William Louis Stern is Chairman of the Department of Botany at the University of Florida, Gainesville.

THE COVER: Three miniature gloxinia plants, snuggled in a 1⅜-inch terra-cotta pot, rest next to a full-sized bloom of a hybrid tea rose. One of the smallest of tropical plants, the miniature gloxinia blooms almost continuously indoors, producing pale flowers on thread-thin stems. Each tiny flower lasts a week or longer.

For information about any Time-Life book, please write:
Reader Information
Time-Life Books
541 North Fairbanks Court
Chicago, Illinois 60611

Library of Congress Cataloguing in Publication Data
Perl, Philip.
    Miniatures and bonsai.
    (The Time-Life encyclopedia of gardening)
    Bibliography: p.
    Includes index.
    1. Miniature plants. 2. Gardens, Miniature.
3. Bonsai. I. Time-Life Books. II. Title.
SB433.5.P39   635.9   78-20889
ISBN 0-8094-2643-9
ISBN 0-8094-2642-0 lib. bdg.
ISBN 0-8094-2641-2 retail ed.

CONTENTS

Gardening on the smallest scale 1

Miniatures in any form have always excited admiration. The ability to create tiny, elaborate figures out of bits of ivory, as in Japanese netsuke carvings, or to capture a scene of glowing splendor in a fraction of a page, as in medieval illuminated manuscripts, is a formidable demonstration of artistic skill. Even in matters that are not so esthetic, miniatures capture attention and excite wonder. About a century ago, a midget named Charles Sherwood Stratton was rechristened Tom Thumb and was exhibited with great success by the legendary circus magnate, P. T. Barnum. To this day, Tom Thumb's stage name is used as a synonym for miniature in the nomenclature of fruits, vegetables and flowers.

This interest in all things extraordinarily small extends logically to miniature plants. Most gardeners are enthralled by tiny rosebuds breathtakingly tinted and furled, growing on bushes only a few inches tall, or by a perfectly formed Tiny Tim tomato less than an inch in diameter, growing on a plant no more than a foot tall and comfortably at home on a dining-room window sill. (The name of the lad who melted Scrooge's heart, Tiny Tim, is almost as ubiquitous in the dubbing of miniature plants as that of Tom Thumb.)

The two kinds of plants that are the subjects of this book—miniatures and dwarfs—share the attribute of smaller-than-expected size. But the diminution of the plants, depending on their original structure, is caused by different processes.

A true miniature bears genes that dictate smallness in all parts of the plant, including its flowers and fruit. Such a plant may originate in the sudden deviation from normal growth found in a bud sport—a mutation due to a spontaneous change within the genes that control its growth. These changes can be occasioned by natural causes, such as ultraviolet light, or man-made causes, such as X-rays. If the change is perpetuated in succeeding generations, a new miniature is born.

A bouquet of miniature zinnias, dahlias, blue leadwort and pearl-like heather nestles in a china teacup. In the foreground are the dainty blossoms of miniature gladiolus (left) and clematis (right).

But there are also true miniatures that have been made small by environmental factors—an alpine plant, for example, that has been growing for many generations on a starvation diet atop a mountain. In this case of survival of the fittest, one that would have delighted Charles Darwin had he gone to the Alps instead of the Galápagos Islands, the genes that cause smallness have become dominant over the genes that commonly dictate largeness. Such a plant will remain small even if it is moved to more favorable growing conditions, and its offspring will be small.

WHAT MAKES A DWARF?

A dwarf plant can usually be distinguished from a true miniature because some parts of it, most often the flowers and fruit, remain full-sized. The most dramatic of the dwarfs are the bonsai, produced not by altering the genetic structure but by confining the plant in a small container with little soil and subjecting it to severe and repeated pruning, especially of the roots.

Nature may similarly stunt a plant with poor growing conditions, but if the plant has not been genetically altered it is likely to prove surprisingly robust in the shelter of a fertile home garden. Still other dwarfs are kept small by grafting, sometimes in dizzying sequence. A dwarf apple tree can consist of a crab apple rootstock, a lower trunk chosen for strength, an upper trunk from a natural dwarf, and finally a top chosen for desirable fruiting qualities.

Plants that are simply the smallest of their kind, such as certain species of the Japanese maple, are often referred to as dwarfs, although their small stature is quite normal. (There is, however, one species of Japanese maple that is a true miniature.) Tiny conifers are also called dwarfs, but in this case the most likely cause of their smallness is genetic mutation. These plants could also properly be called miniatures.

CHERISHING TININESS

Small plants have been treasured for at least 2,000 years; dwarf pines and junipers were respected symbols of age in China by the First Century A.D. Their popularity in the West is centered among the many gardeners who treasure beautiful tiny things— people who might be collecting stamps or furnishing dollhouses if they were not busy cultivating, say, a Jones columbine 2 inches tall with ½-inch blue or purple flowers and ⅓-inch spurs. With a judicious selection of miniatures and dwarfs, it is possible to create the impression of an acre of garden in a space only 20 feet square or to reproduce the rose garden of Malmaison in a living room.

In the years following World War II, the use of miniatures and dwarfs as house and garden plants has steadily increased in response to what seems to be a shrinking environment. As living space becomes the ultimate luxury, small plants make the best use of it.

A garden so small that it affords neighborly conversations over the back fence, common in the housing developments of densely populated areas, is no place for a grove of tall pine trees or a conventional fruit orchard. But by skillfully positioning dwarf and miniature trees, shrubs and flowers, an illusion of vast space can be achieved. A yard that is too cramped to admit two standard apple trees will accommodate a pair of dwarfs in one sixth the space the full-sized trees would need. This pair of dwarf trees, properly cared for, can produce a harvest of more than 500 pounds of fruit between them every year.

Even more pressed to make the most of space is the landless city dweller, especially one whose apartment may have only a single exposure to daylight. A window sill that holds but three standard-sized house plants will accommodate up to three dozen miniature plants in 2-inch pots, greatly expanding the potential for variety and experimentation.

VARIETY BY THE DOZEN

Such miniatures need not be confined to a window sill. They can be displayed anywhere there is a bit of space. If daylight is as limited as space, their need for supplemental light is modest. A dozen miniature begonias, for example, can be comfortably lighted with a single 15-watt fluorescent tube only 18 inches long.

Several true miniatures—those with genes that dictate smallness—have been known for centuries. One is *Rosa rouletii,* only two inches tall, which was found growing in a pot in a remote village in the Swiss Alps in 1917. It had been rather taken for granted until it was propagated in England by plantsman Henry Correvon, who created a boom in miniature roses in Europe and the United States. Unlike the Swiss villagers, contemporary hybridizers are not content to keep on growing the same old sports. They have industriously produced more than 700 varieties of miniature roses by crossbreeding miniatures with conventional roses that had such desirable qualities as a wide range of color or exceptional form. When necessary, the resulting hybrid is grafted onto a dwarfing rootstock, as is done with apple trees, to make sure the new plant will remain small.

The job of hybridizing is extraordinarily complex because most plants are polygenic; that is, each has many genes that are involved in controlling size. The rate of success among rose breeders seeking new miniatures is only one in 30,000 seedlings.

SEEDS OR CUTTINGS

Once a true miniature is found or developed and the size is stabilized, the plant can be propagated by seed and the offspring will have the parent's smallness characteristic. This is standard practice with quick-growing miniature vegetables. With slow-growing woody plants, it is not necessary for growers to wait through several

The highs and lows of plants

A plant's pattern of growth is determined primarily by its genetic heritage and its environment. Genes establish what a plant can do under the best of circumstances; environment—including intervention by man—determines what it may do under any circumstances. Very favorable growing conditions can push a plant to the upper limits of its genetic capacity; harsh living conditions can stunt it. Culturally induced characteristics are neither permanent nor hereditary. An apple tree dwarfed by repeated pruning will shoot back to normal size if pruning is stopped, and its seeds will produce normal-sized offspring.

For any characteristic to be passed on to successive generations, a plant must undergo a genetic change, through evolution, mutation *(opposite page),* or hybridization. The genetic heritage of a plant is so complex that some characteristics may change while others, seemingly related, will not. Thus, a genetically dwarfed tomato plant may bear standard-sized fruit. This reduced height can be passed on through cuttings and, once the change is stabilized, through seeds.

Sizing up plant growth

STANDARD
A standard plant will usually reach the genetically determined height typical of its species, establishing norms for the size of leaves, flowers and fruit, the length of internodes (the spaces between bulging nodes on stems or branches) and rate of growth.

COMPACT
A compact plant is shorter and slower-growing than the standard, but its internodes, leaves and flowers are usually full sized. This partial growth reduction may be caused by mutation of a few genes or by unfavorable conditions.

DWARF
Although a dwarf plant usually has standard-sized leaves, flowers and fruit, it is shorter, grows more slowly than a compact plant of its species, and has shorter internodes. This stunting can be caused by the mutation of several genes, or by severe cultural handicaps such as poor growing conditions, induced early flowering (which leads a plant to mature sooner), forced horizontal branching (which slows growth) or extensive and repeated pruning. Such culturally induced dwarfing is not permanent, nor will it be passed on to the next generation.

MINIATURE
A miniature plant not only has a slow growth rate and short internodes, but its leaves, flowers and fruit are in scale with its reduced height. This is because a major genetic change has occurred within the plant. Unlike a culturally induced dwarf, a miniature will not revert to standard size, and its offspring will also be miniatures.

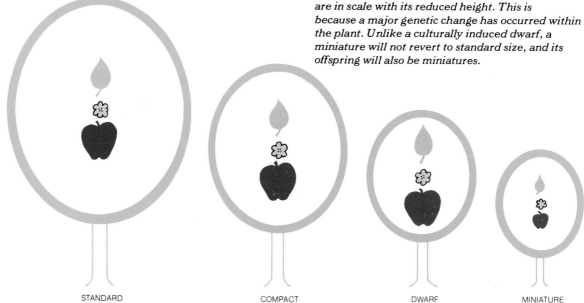

STANDARD   COMPACT   DWARF   MINIATURE

THE BEGINNINGS OF GROWTH

Growth in both plants and animals depends on cell division. In plants, this takes place primarily at the tips of roots and stems, although it also occurs in young leaves, fruit and seeds. The process begins when the threadlike chromosomes in a dividing cell's nucleus become sausage-shaped (right).

HOW MUTATIONS OCCUR

The chromosomes contain a full set of the plant's heredity units, or genes, one for every characteristic of the plant. Within a single chromosome there are as many as 3,000 genes. In normal cell division, each chromosome and its genes split into two identical parts. But sometimes things go awry and the structure of the chromosome is altered. This change, a mutation, is most often caused by invisible light—an ultraviolet ray, x-ray or gamma ray—striking the cell while it is dividing. Mutation may affect the interrelationship of the genes, making recessive ones suddenly dominant. The more genes affected by mutation, the greater the changes in the plant.

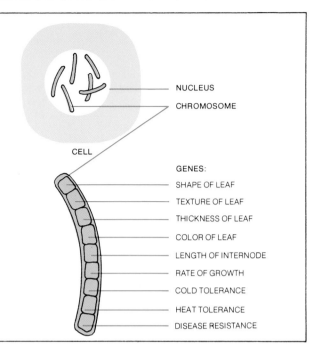

NUCLEUS
CHROMOSOME
CELL

GENES:
SHAPE OF LEAF
TEXTURE OF LEAF
THICKNESS OF LEAF
COLOR OF LEAF
LENGTH OF INTERNODE
RATE OF GROWTH
COLD TOLERANCE
HEAT TOLERANCE
DISEASE RESISTANCE

Characteristics of a miniature

NODE
INTERNODE
NODE
INTERNODE

SHORT INTERNODES

The internodes—the distances between a plant's bulging stem nodes—are shorter in a miniature plant than in a standard plant of the same kind, because of a genetic mutation. Shorter internodes can also appear in a dwarf plant, caused by cultural manipulations.

SMALL LEAVES

The leaves of a miniature plant are markedly smaller and often more indented than those of its standard counterpart. These changes also result from a genetic mutation. Slightly smaller leaves can appear on a dwarf plant grown in poor or shallow soil, or if it undergoes leaf stripping—a practice that forces the growth of smaller leaves on some deciduous trees.

SMALL FLOWERS

Unlike its dwarf cousins, a miniature plant has smaller flowers than those of the standard counterpart. This change is genetically dictated. Although horticulturists have been able to grow larger flowers on some plants by pinching off all but a few buds, their efforts to find a cultural or nongenetic way to reduce flower size have been unsuccessful.

SMALL FRUIT

A miniature, unlike a dwarf plant, produces smaller fruit than a standard plant of the same kind. This reduction, like a reduction in flower size, is genetically caused and cannot be duplicated culturally. In a miniature calamondin orange (far right), the gene for seed size has not been altered, so the tiny fruit contains seeds like those of a standard-sized orange.

11

Nature makes a miniature

When a mutation occurs in a cell of an emerging bud, the branch that sprouts there may be genetically different from the rest of the plant. Miniature roses are believed to have evolved from such bud mutations, called sports (right). But not all bud mutations result in miniatures: the first navel orange appeared on a sport. So did the first nectarine—essentially a peach without fuzz—which grew from a sport on a peach tree.

BUD SPORT

Man makes a hybrid miniature

A tomato plant has either determinate or indeterminate growing tips. The former type bears fruit both along its side shoots and at the tip of its stem, which stops its growth (right). The latter bears fruit only along the side shoots; its tip keeps growing until the plant is killed by frost (far right). It takes several crossings of the smallest possible determinate-type plant with the smallest possible small-fruited plant to create a hybrid with tiny tomatoes and limited size.

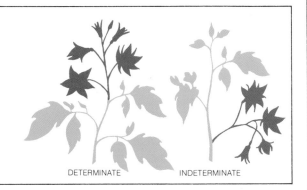

DETERMINATE   INDETERMINATE

Man-made dwarfs

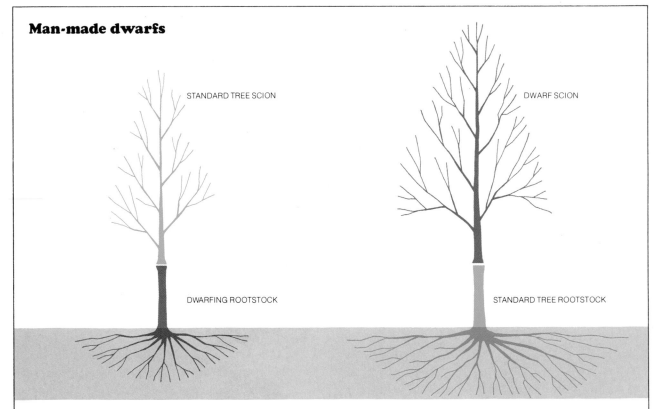

STANDARD TREE SCION

DWARF SCION

DWARFING ROOTSTOCK

STANDARD TREE ROOTSTOCK

The dwarf fruit tree you buy at a local nursery is most likely parts of two trees, a dwarf and a standard, grafted together. A dwarf scion with superior fruit, grafted onto a hardy, disease-resistant standard rootstock, will produce a tree shorter than a standard fruit tree (right). But it will not be as short as a standard scion grafted onto a dwarfing rootstock (left). In either case, the grafted tree demands less space than a standard tree; it bears fruit within two years of planting, several years ahead of a standard; and the fruit will be as large as, or larger than, that of a standard and often sweeter.

generations to stabilize the dwarfness. These miniature plants can be multiplied vegetatively, using rooted cuttings. Each will produce an exact duplicate of the original and each becomes a potential source of more cuttings. Some plants, including many evergreens, are difficult or impossible to start from cuttings. In such a case, the cuttings are grafted onto nurse rootstocks that simply provide them with nourishment without affecting size.

Bonsai trees, miniature in size but not in genes, require the daily ministrations of an attentive gardener in order to remain alive and healthy under stringent growing conditions. In addition to severe root pruning, auxiliary techniques are used to control size. One such refinement is leaf stripping, a delicate process in which leaves considered too large for a tree are removed. On a few kinds of trees, this initiates the growth of a second set of smaller leaves. This works well for leaves but, despite the best efforts of many generations of plant experts, the fruits and flowers of bonsai remain maddeningly full-sized. During all the centuries of bonsai culture, nobody has yet managed to make them respond to the otherwise successful principles of growth stunting.

For impatient bonsai growers unwilling to wait several hundred years for a bonsai to be old, it is important that it at least look old. The things that can be done to give the appearance of age are a sort of reverse cosmetology. Some branches and a portion of the trunk are stripped of their bark to expose the wood beneath, suggesting that lightning had struck a tall, old tree. Brushing the exposed wood with diluted household bleach eventually silvers it to look like driftwood. The pencil-thin trunk of a young tree is thickened to thumb-size and tapered to suggest that of an older one by constant pruning and pinching back. Copper wire is spiraled around branches to shape them into desired configurations, but despite a general belief to the contrary, the wire does not serve as a corset to constrict growth. In fact, if the wire seems to be cutting into the bark, it should be removed immediately before it creates unsightly furrows.

Some 2,000 years ago, wealthy Chinese began to decorate their courtyards with plants growing in containers. Some of these plants were individually potted trees and shrubs, while others included several plants and some rocks—miniature gardens much like those that are so popular today. All were known as *p'en-jing*—meaning "scene in a tray."

The concept of such potted plants as decoration arrived in Japan shortly after the introduction of Buddhism from China in the Sixth Century A.D.; the earliest pictorial record appears in an 1195 scroll depicting the life of a priest named Saigyo, a member of the

IMITATIONS OF AGE

privileged class that adopted potted plants not only as a hobby but as a symbol of status.

In the centuries that followed, the art of dwarfing potted plants and prolonging their lives gradually evolved, influenced by the contemplative nature of Zen Buddhism along the way. But the name bonsai, meaning "to cultivate in a tray," came into use less than 300 years ago as a substitute for more cumbersome terms after the art became popular among large numbers of people. In the burst of enthusiasm that followed, virtually all of the interesting-shaped small trees growing wild in Japan were uprooted and converted into bonsai. The practice was subsequently prohibited, but few such trees can be found to this day.

BONSAI MOVES ABROAD

The opening of Japan to the West by Commodore Matthew Perry in 1854 brought to many Westerners their first exposure to bonsai. Early in the present century, Japanese bonsai were shown at fairs and exhibitions in many of the major cities of the United States and Europe, and fascination with the small trees has never flagged. On the occasion of the United States Bicentennial celebration in 1976, the gift of the Japanese people to America was a magnificent bonsai collection, including trees ranging in age up to 350 years; the collection is now on permanent display at the National Arboretum in Washington, D.C.

While all bonsai are dwarfed, not all dwarf trees are bonsai. Those that are not differ from the carefully tended bonsai in that they are simply slow-growing, either naturally or as a result of grafting. A Norway spruce that could be expected to tower 150 feet above the ground at maturity might, in dwarf form, become only six or seven feet tall. Such freaks, mutations resulting from altered genes, appear rather often. In a forest they would die from lack of sunlight, but horticulturists have propagated dwarfs of almost all the tall coniferous evergreens. Seeds of many of these mutations come from the so-called witches' brooms, ragged clusters of twigs and branches that you see in big evergreen trees, looking like huge, sloppy birds' nests.

GRAFTED APPLE TREES

Similarly stunted fruit trees, natural dwarfs, have been grown as novelties for some 300 years. In 1912, horticulturists in England found that a standard apple tree, when grafted onto the roots or lower trunk of a selected species of a naturally dwarfed apple tree, would itself become dwarfed. As a result gardeners have a wide choice of grafted apple trees that grow only 8 or 10 feet tall instead of 25 but bear full-sized, extra-sweet fruits.

Pear trees are usually dwarfed by being grafted onto quince rootstocks, and peach trees are grafted onto bush cherries or plums.

Although dwarf-plum-tree roots are sturdy enough to support peaches, they are not sufficient for plums themselves, so standard plum trees must be grafted onto bush cherries to be dwarfed. And the bush cherry, despite its success with other fruits, is a failure with other cherries, which continue to tower two or three feet over the dwarfed trees of other fruits in the garden.

When it comes to flowers, the term dwarf is even more loosely used. It generally denotes plants that are short in relation to the normal size of the species but nonetheless yield full-sized flowers, as is the case with dwarf trees that bear full-sized fruits. But dwarf marigolds, to cite one example, can produce blooms only 1½ inches wide on stems a mere seven inches tall. By comparison, the giant among the standard marigolds, the African species, can tower 3 feet high and bear globe-shaped blossoms that are 5 inches in diameter. So even if the dwarf marigolds are only termed "extra dwarf" in the seed catalogue, they will perform as miniatures for the space-shy gardener. Some plants, the dahlia for example, are notoriously unstable genetically; just when plant breeders think a miniature has been stabilized, it is likely to produce an even smaller version, creating a dilemma of nomenclature. What should a miniature of a miniature be called?

VEGETABLE MIDGETS

In the case of vegetables, American seedsmen have shown no such reluctance to call a miniature a miniature. They have developed or imported a wide range of midget vegetables, from snow peas to tiny watermelons to sweet corn—the latter bearing ears only five inches long. Even smaller ears of baby corn—perfectly formed but only one inch long and one quarter inch wide—are occasionally served in expensive Chinese dishes; they are canned in the Orient and exported to the United States. The fascination of such miniatures of familiar foods is hardly in their economy, since a single standard carrot will provide more carrot to eat than the eight or ten midgets that might have been grown in its place. But no one can deny the gourmet appeal of eating such miniatures as *petits pois* or *fraises des bois* rather than regular garden peas or strawberries.

A number of miniature vegetables were developed in Holland, including the Spinel beet, one inch in diameter at maturity, and the Sucram carrot, not quite as thick as the Spinel beet and only five inches long. In the United States, some miniatures have been developed to satisfy particularly local needs; one such is the Minnesota Midget, a baseball-sized cantaloupe that ripens in 60 days rather than the 90 usually needed for larger varieties. This lets the fruit come in safely before the first autumn frost in a state where winter arrives early and stays late.

Manipulating growth

Gardener-controlled methods of dwarfing a plant are based on interfering with its natural hormonal guidance system or with the flow of nutrients between its roots and shoots. The plant's growth slows when it sidetracks energy in an attempt to restore a normal growth pattern. The control techniques illustrated can be used in combination if you do not apply them too severely during any one growing season. Your aim is to slow growth, not stop it altogether. If you halt the manipulations, the plant will revert to normal growth and ultimately reach its standard size and shape.

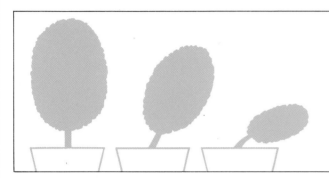

ANGLES THAT INFLUENCE SIZE

Stems, branches and shoots of most plants, guided by hormones, grow up toward life-giving light. The farther such plants are bent from a vertical axis toward the horizontal (or even below the horizontal), the more their growth rate slows. New growth along the bent member will try to turn upward. Judicious pruning when this happens keeps the plant at the desired height.

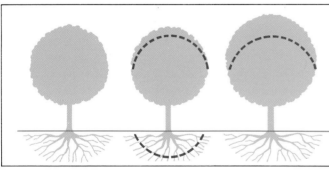

NUTRITION TOP TO BOTTOM

Every plant balances its root structure with its top growth. When branches are pruned off, a corresponding section of roots must also be removed, or vice versa, to maintain this balance. If only the top is pruned, roots send up more nutrients than the top needs, forcing it into more vigorous growth than ever. Limiting soil and fertilizer also helps to dwarf top growth.

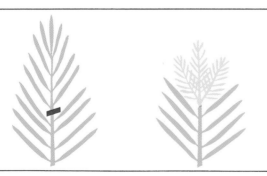

A TIP ON EVERGREENS

If the soft new growth of evergreens with branches growing in whorls is pinched off just above the dormant buds below it, these buds will develop. The tip produced inhibiting hormones that kept the buds dormant. The plant now directs its energy to these buds, and several shoots appear. New growth will be shorter than usual, and older branches will thicken.

DECIDUOUS DWARFING

Pinching off new growth on deciduous plants just above dormant buds will force these buds to emerge by diverting energy that would have gone into the single shoot. The replacement shoots have a shorter growing season, so new growth will be shorter and, again, old growth will thicken. Pruning the replacement shoots more during the season dwarfs the plant even more severely.

Sometimes a reduction in size can have unexpected advantages. A watermelon such as the New Hampshire Midget, only seven inches long and about as wide, is easier to fit into a refrigerator than a standard watermelon, or into a plastic-foam box to keep it cold for a picnic. The Cheyenne pumpkin, which was developed on the ranges of Wyoming, is but six inches high; carved into a jack-o'-lantern, it sits comfortably on a window sill at Halloween.

The early history of miniatures other than bonsai is sparsely documented, largely because no one took them very seriously until gardeners and collectors created a demand for them. Some believe that miniature roses originated in China, along with such familiar products as firecrackers and spaghetti pasta, and were taken to Europe by 19th Century traders. But others believe that *Rosa rouletii,* at least, originated in the Alps.

Whatever the truth, by the end of the 19th Century the long-standing hybridizing notion that bigger is better was beginning to be challenged in England. In *The Growth of Gardening,* Richard Gorer quotes an indignant John Walsh, who protested thus in 1870:

"The fuchsia has suffered a terrible degradation within the past few years, for almost every addition to the lists of new sorts has been an addition to the family of monsters of hideous mien. The corollas have expanded more and more, until what was once like a cup, a goblet or a Rhine wine glass, has become at last a flat disc or a miniature washing tub, a shameful mockery of all our pretentions. It is a dispiriting reflexion on public taste that a plant so renowned for grace has become in the hands of certain florists a very type of deformity."

Credit for the early development of hybridized miniatures must accrue to a Dutch commercial grower, Jan de Vink, who had less than one acre of land to his name. De Vink was the first hybridizer to apply pollen from standard roses to *Rosa rouletii* to see what would happen. What happened initially was the development of the famous red miniature, Tom Thumb, which arrived in the United States in 1934 and became the first patented miniature rose in this country in 1936.

A short time later, an American hybridizer named Bruce Williamson, working in Indiana, introduced a so-called table iris, later to be known as the miniature *tall* bearded iris. In the 1950s, the miniature *dwarf* bearded iris arrived on the scene, developed by Indiana's Walter Welch and Paul Cook. Soon such plants entered horticultural lists and catalogues, and thus began the complex, often confusing but always intriguing nomenclature process that still prevails in the world of miniatures.

The spellbinding beauty of tiny roses

Brought from China by early traders, miniature roses, with their exquisitely formed flowers, were the rage of aristocratic Europe during the late 18th and early 19th Centuries. They were dubbed fairy roses and cast a spell that even transcended war. Napoleon, during his quarrels with England, granted free passage to any English horticulturist who brought new rose miniatures into France for Empress Josephine's gardens.

European infatuation with miniature roses subsided during the Victorian era when tastes turned toward the larger hybrid perpetual roses, but interest revived in 1918 when the tiny *rouletii* rose (*page 9*) was discovered growing in a Swiss Alpine village. "This is the most Lilliputian of all roses," wrote one of its enthusiastic discoverers, Henry Correvon. "It flowers perpetually, and I have just been out to gather buds from under the snow covering my garden."

The continuing popularity of tiny replicas of hybrid tea and floribunda roses now seems assured. Hundreds of bush and climbing miniatures have been registered with the American Rose Society, and more hybrids are being added each year. Unlike most other modern roses, miniatures are grown on their own roots. They range in height from the tiny Si, about 4 inches tall, to the bushy Lavender Lace, up to 18 inches high. Some climbing hybrids, such as Red Cascade, will trail along the ground, if unsupported, to a distance of 6 to 8 feet. Most miniatures bloom profusely from spring to frost, producing dime- to quarter-sized blooms in a joyful range of colors as varied as those of their large cousins.

Despite their delicate appearance, miniature roses are strong, versatile plants. They can be grown outdoors in pots, window boxes, rock gardens, hanging baskets or as an edging for a rose border. Indoors, they will bloom every six to eight weeks if placed on a sunny window sill or under artificial light. Miniatures require the same care as other roses—well-drained, slightly acid soil and plenty of sunshine and humidity. If given these conditions they will readily reproduce the flowers that once enchanted an empress.

Each jewel-like scarlet bloom of Midget,
the miniature rose in the foreground, could
rest on a single petal of the floribunda
rose Bonfire Night, in the background.

Miniature roses edge a bed of large floribundas and hybrid teas. The wood-chip mulch conserves moisture and regulates soil

temperature for the miniatures' shallow roots. The tiny red blooms at right belong to a climbing miniature, Madelyn Lang.

Life-sized portraits: the bush miniatures

GLORIGLO: *This rose blooms at intervals from spring until frost.*

STARINA: *Less hardy than most other miniatures, it grows up to 18 inches in height.*

SIMPLEX: *The buds are apricot in color, but the flowers are creamy white.*

OVER THE RAINBOW: *Its three-toned flowers appear on prostrate bushes 12 to 14 inches wide.*

FAIRY ROSE: *The pink-tinged flowers of this miniature grow in eye-catching clusters.*

MAGIC CARROUSEL: *With a whirl of color, this rose aptly reflects its name.*

RISE 'N' SHINE: *Boasting large, bushy foliage, it grows to a height of 15 to 24 inches.*

BEAUTY SECRET: *The bright high-centered flowers have a strong fragrance.*

TOM THUMB: *In 1936, it became the first patented miniature rose.*

BONNY: *Its long-lasting flowers are staged against a backdrop of red-tinted foliage.*

ROULETII: *This vigorous rose is the parent of many modern miniatures.*

Life-sized portraits: the climbing miniatures

PINK CAMEO: *A vigorous hybrid, it produces small clusters of rosy flowers.*

MADELYN LANG: *Trained on a trellis, it will climb to a height of 5 feet or more.*

JEANNE LAJOIE: *It resembles a larger relative, a hybrid tea rose.*

HI HO: *Its showy multipetaled flowers bloom outdoors until frost.*

The prodigal miniature climbing rose Jeanne Lajoie creates a blush of color against the dark wood of a fence. In the foreground are the large blooms of Red Lion, a hybrid tea.

Growing up small in the great indoors 2

With the tiny yet perfectly formed and tinted flowers of a Wee Lass African violet or a dollhouse-sized basket of miniature maidenhair ferns, you can weave your own indoor world of fact and fancy. Tempted by the tropics? Slip a small creeping fig into a seashell. If your tastes run to the austere, a miniature rebutia in a 2-inch pot will bring a suggestion of the arid desert into an apartment living room. Whether you are potting a single plant or creating a minor universe, scale and proportion are especially important in these tiny compositions. A fragile wine goblet, for example, lends itself more readily to a delicate flowering sinningia than to a stubby cactus; a cactus looks best if it has a lot of elbow room in a rugged pottery container.

Once you begin, be forewarned: the temptation will be to plant every little container you find around the house. But keep in mind that the smidgeon of soil in thimble-sized pots dries out very quickly. Thus, the general rule for watering most miniatures in small containers with or without drainage holes is to do so sparingly but often. For the rest, growing miniatures is as easy as growing any other house plant once you know a plant's basic needs: whether it prefers acid or alkaline soil, shade or direct sunlight, lots of humidity or drier air.

A simple way to begin is with plants that flower generously, are easy to raise, and whose familiar full-sized versions give you an idea of what to expect. Miniature begonias, African violets and geraniums all prefer slightly acid soil that is a mixture of one part each of peat moss, potting soil and builder's sand (beach sand is too salty). Peat moss not only adds acidity to the soil but helps to retain moisture—a vital consideration in this enterprise. Still, adequate drainage is also important, except in the tiniest of pots, which, as noted, tend to dry out quickly and have no space for drainage material. When there is room, put down a layer of sand or tiny pebbles, leaving space for the potting mix and the plant's root ball. Follow this with small bits of charcoal to keep the soil fresh. Add the

Miniature African violets, planted in 2- and 2¼-inch pots, line the upper two shelves of a window garden. Below, standard-sized African violets rest on a tray of pebbles moistened to help maintain humidity.

soil and then the plant, pressing it gently into its new home with your finger tips or the rubber end of a pencil. If you moisten the root ball and the soil before planting, you will only need to sprinkle a bit of water from an eyedropper to settle the soil.

A TENDER MOVE   Without sacrificing gentle handling, try to work as quickly as possible when you are transplanting these miniatures. Their tiny roots will dry out unless you have everything ready for their move before you unpot them. For the same reason, avoid transplanting them in bright sunlight. And for the first month or so, do not fertilize a newly potted plant; it needs a chance to heal and recuperate, not a sudden jolt of stimulation that might burn its tender tissues. The key to fertilizing miniatures is to do so sparingly if you want the plant to remain very small. The nutrients in the small amount of soil in a tiny pot will be used up in time, however, and will need boosting at least each spring. If the pot has no drainage hole, fertilizer salts will accumulate, making it necessary to repot the plant with fresh soil. Be sure to dilute the fertilizer to one quarter the strength recommended on the label to avoid burning the roots. Miniature African violets need to be fed more frequently, with almost every watering, using ¼ teaspoon of African violet plant food per gallon of water; flush out fertilizer salts with plain water every third or fourth watering.

Violets and geraniums will grow contentedly in 2-inch pots for several years without showing signs of claustrophobia, but begonias are rather less docile and will need to be moved along to larger quarters in a year or two. The African violets need indirect or curtain-filtered light, the begonias need sun in winter but will benefit if light is gently shaded for them in summer, and the geraniums grow best in as much sunlight as you can provide. Temperatures of about 75° by day and 65° at night should suit them all, as should soil that is kept evenly moist. One gardener likens perfect soil to perfect chocolate cake: neither dry and stale nor heavy and soggy, but nicely moist and crumbly.

MOISTURIZING PLATFORM   Perhaps even more than their larger cousins these tiny plants must be given adequate humidity. One way to raise the humidity and lower your watering chores is to group several small pots on a dish or tray filled with gravel that is kept wet. To unify a disconnected array of small pots, you might keep them in a muffin tin in which gravel has been substituted for batter, and place the tin inside a decorative rectangular wicker basket. Beware of overcrowding, however; plants require good air circulation to prevent attacks of fungus and other diseases. And a weekly grooming to remove dead leaves not only makes for a tidier display but also prevents accumulated foliage from rotting.

For variety—and a delightful fragrance—consider adding a miniature orchid, *Neofinetia falcata,* to the communal muffin tin. On plants that are two or four inches high, neofinetia produces sprays of tiny white sweet-smelling flowers. The orchid should be potted in a clay container, whose porous sides will allow the plant's roots access to needed oxygen. A planting mix of shredded fir bark, redwood bark, perlite and coarse peat moss will provide added air circulation. Do make certain, if you are grouping orchids on a tray, that they are not standing in water; they will survive dryness more easily than excessive wetness.

Another way to grow miniature flowers—and to perk up a dreary January—is to prepare a pan of dwarf bulbs in September or

REPOTTING A MINIATURE

1. *To repot a tiny plant in a smaller container, turn it upside down and slide it out of its original pot. Gently crumble away enough soil from around the root ball so it will fit loosely in its new holder.*

2. *For fit, you may need to cut some roots off. Snip off a proportionate amount of top growth, using tiny scissors. If the container is cup-sized or larger and has no drainage hole, put in ¼ inch of coarse sand to absorb excess water. Fill the bottom quarter of any container with potting soil laced with a pinch of charcoal dust.*

3. *Use the blade of an old table knife to firm potting soil around the roots so there are no air spaces, adding soil as needed with a teaspoon. The base of the plant's stem should be ⅛ inch below the container rim. Water sparingly with an eyedropper or teaspoon.*

4. *Cover the transplant with a plastic bag to retain moisture. Support the bag with a stick and leave it open at the bottom. Set the plant in a cool, bright place away from direct sunlight. In two or three days, remove the bag; keep the soil moist but not soggy thereafter. Soil dries quickly in tiny containers.*

October. You might use a soup bowl or a clay saucer as the container. The bulbs should not touch each other, but they are so small— perhaps an inch in diameter—that several of them will fit without overcrowding into a soup bowl. Since you are using a container that does not have a drainage hole, start with a shallow layer of gravel mixed with powdered charcoal. The potting soil should be the kind that is sold for African violets; use it to fill the container to within ½ inch of the rim. The bulbs should then be set into the soil with the rounded side downward and the narrower end up *(opposite page)*. Moisten the soil carefully. To keep the moisture in, mulch the surface and wrap the entire pan in plastic film that has two or three small holes punched in it.

Next, to ensure that the potted and watered bulbs form a good root system, chill them in a refrigerator, at temperatures between 40 and 50 degrees, for four to 15 weeks, depending on the kind of bulb. If you have no space in your refrigerator, an unheated garage should do. Test the soil occasionally to be sure it has not dried out. To force growth and bloom, move the chilled bulbs into a shady place at room temperature for one day, then set them on a sunny window sill. Once bloom is achieved, keep plants as cool as possible, especially at night. With this treatment you can have a cheerful 10-day display of such lovelies as Hoop Petticoat daffodils, whose golden yellow ¾-inch blooms appear on plants that grow 6 to 8 inches high, or Angel's Tears daffodils, with clusters of 1-inch creamy white flowers on 6-inch stalks. When your winter wonders have faded, you may save the bulbs for fall planting outdoors, where they will bloom again the following spring.

CREATING DISH GARDENS

From pans of bulbs and communal muffin tins of violets and begonias, it is but a small step to the creation of a miniature garden or a landscape-in-a-dish. Here again, scale and composition are important concerns. The garden on your coffee table will be subject to detailed inspection, so the "trees" grown from a miniature holly must be in proportion to the baby's tears that provides your green meadow. As with any garden, the living things you gather together must share similar growing requirements, especially in their need for moisture. Even if a tropical plant looks compatible with a cactus, one would have to be sacrificed to the other's survival. One avid dish gardener—who swears she began grouping plants only "so I'd have fewer pots to water"—now finds herself creating small-scale botanical exhibits. "The more gardens I put together," she says, "the more interested I am in designing them well. And the more I pay attention to the natural habitats of plants, their cultural requirements, the way they live in nature." When in doubt, keep the plantings within the same family; you will have no trouble finding a wide variety even with that limitation.

An easy initiation into miniature landscapes is a rock garden with a desert theme. A simple clay saucer at least 3 inches deep, of the kind placed under tall house plants, will do for a container (desert plants grow better in porous clay pots because they are adapted to dry conditions). First put down a layer of gravel ½ inch thick for drainage, followed by a mixture of equal parts of builder's sand and potting soil. To neutralize the acidity of the potting soil, add a tablespoon of ground limestone to the soil in each container. You may want to pile some of the soil slightly higher at one end to add a touch of landscaping interest. The almost weightless chunks of volcanic rock that are available in most garden-supply centers, or any rugged-looking stones you can find, will make fine boulders. Arrange them in an informal design, perhaps adding a piece of bleached driftwood in one corner or a trickle of white gravel to simulate a dry gulch.

Miniature cacti and succulents come in a wide range of shapes, colors and textures. You might contrast the columnar succulent peperomia, 6 inches tall, with the squattiness of a pincushion cactus or the smooth, shiny ground-hugging rosettes of an echevaria. Cacti have shallow root systems, so pack them into the soil gently but firmly. Finally, give your mini-Mojave as much warmth and sunshine as you can.

For an inviting mountain scene, use a soil mix of potting soil, peat moss, sand and crushed limestone in equal parts. Bits of tile or

TO DRESS A DESERT

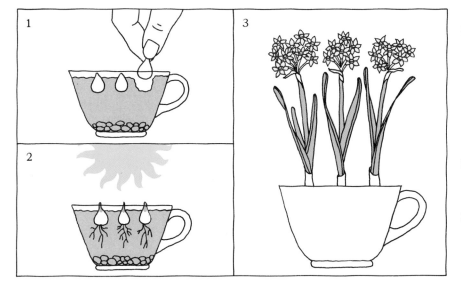

FORCING BLOOMS IN WINTER

1. *For winter flowers from spring-flowering bulbs, prepare a container with pebbles and potting soil. Space bulbs ½ inch apart, setting tiny varieties ½ inch deep and burying larger ones up to the neck. Keep the soil moist. Chill the potted bulbs in a refrigerator at 40° for eight weeks or more.*

2. *Move the pot to a sunny window sill after keeping it at room temperature for one day.*

3. *To prolong flower life, keep open blooms in indirect light. After foliage dies the bulbs can be replanted outdoors, where they will bloom on their normal schedule.*

gravel can be used to make a winding path to the top of a hill that you have covered with a spreading miniature harebell; it will fill your tray with a shallow mat of greenery, above which, all summer long, will float clusters of bell-shaped florets the color of faded denim. Tiny saxifrages share a need for bright light with the harebell, and several varieties mixed with the harebells will dot the landscape in February and March with buttery yellow flowers like lily trumpets merely ¼ inch wide.

INDOOR ROSE GARDENS

Having made the desert and the mountain bloom, you may find yourself seeking a greater challenge than informal plantings can provide. Move on, then, to a tiny formal garden of miniature roses. Prepare your container as you did for the mountain garden, omitting the crushed limestone, since roses prefer a more neutral soil, and leaving the surface level. Lay out some angular gravel paths and border them with a few miniature roses chosen for their color and blooming habits *(Chapter 5)*. The plants need at least eight inches between them to avoid crowding. Somewhat startling but nonetheless harmonious color accents can be achieved with Lavender Lace, a sweet-smelling violet rose that grows 12 to 15 inches tall, and Green Ice, whose pink buds open into green-flushed white flowers 1½ inches in diameter.

To plant a miniature rose, free the root ball from the original pot and bury it up to the crown in its new garden. Water thoroughly and move the container to a cool, shaded place for a few days before moving it into the sun. Keep the soil moist but not soggy (remember that perfect chocolate cake), and fertilize monthly with a weak solution of fish emulsion; one teaspoonful per cup of water will serve a dozen miniature roses. Remove faded flowers promptly and keep the bushes pinched back by half, making the cuts at leaf nodes. Though this may seem ruthless to the uninitiated, roses flower most freely on new growth, and this cutting back will increase their flower production as well as improve the general appearance of your tidy little formal garden.

SIMULATING A LAWN

Such a formal garden would not be worthy of its name without some sweeping greenswards. You can fill the open spaces of your portable courtyard with woolly thyme. It will spread to form a carpet two inches high and will bear tiny pink flowers in July. If the leaves become too thickly matted, pinch a few of them off and toss them into your next stew.

Whatever your choice of garden, the whole idea is to keep the plants small. Thus, fertilizing is not usually practiced (except as noted for the roses). But a teaspoonful of bone meal sprinkled lightly will perk up soil that may have become exhausted over a long period of time. Otherwise, moistening the garden about twice a week, keeping it cool, and removing specimens that grow too exuberantly will be the extent of your gardening chores.

If even this much watering seems an onerous task, consider the advantages of growing your miniatures in a closed terrarium. Theoretically, this ecosystem needs no watering at all once you have set the cycle in motion. Practically speaking, however, most plants need some air circulation. That means leaving the cover off the terrarium at least some of the time, and that means a certain amount of water will evaporate, requiring periodic replacement. Ideally, there should be just the slightest condensation on the inside of the glass, not enough to obscure your view of the plants, but enough to ensure that the cycle is functioning.

Any clear glass or plastic container, from pickle jars to water coolers, will make a perfect terrarium. Avoid darkly tinted glass, no matter how handsome the bottle, as it keeps out too much light. Place an inch of gravel at the bottom of the terrarium for drainage, using a funnel if the neck of the container is narrow, and repeat the process with a thin layer of crushed charcoal to keep this microcosm sweet smelling. Then add a thick layer of the basic soil mixture, creating various levels by shoring up soil with volcanic rock or a piece of bark or wood. A plantlet of needlepoint ivy placed high on a slope will send a trail of inch-wide leaves downhill, perhaps to meet the silvery gleam of a miniature aluminum plant or the heart-shaped leaves of prostrate peperomia.

BOTTLE PLANTING

One plant that seems to have been designed especially for terrarium gardeners is *Sinningia pusilla*. These lovely, minuscule gloxinias will produce an almost continuous display of tiny lavender ear trumpets with creamy white or pale yellow throats on plants that are only two inches tall.

The terrarium should be kept at room temperatures that avoid extremes of heat and cold and should receive indirect light (if it is placed in direct sunlight, your little world may accidentally cook itself). Be sure to keep the sinningias picked clean of faded flowers to prevent them from rotting in the humid atmosphere. Use small scissors to clip the plants; fingers are generally too clumsy for tending these fragile tubers.

Some miniatures combine small stature with edibility, not a bad bargain for some enterprising kitchen gardener. But you can't expect to grow even midget vegetables in sinningia-sized pots; you will need containers at least 5 inches wide. To the basic soil mixture of equal parts potting soil, peat moss and sand, add a tablespoon of bone meal per pot, blending it in thoroughly. It will supply adequate

TINY TIMS FOR CHRISTMAS

1. *To raise tomatoes such as the Tiny Tim variety for Christmas, on September 15 make a hole for each seed in a mix of potting soil, peat moss and vermiculite. Cover with mix, water, then cover with a plastic bag. Place in a sunny spot with temperatures from 60° at night to 75° during the day. When the seeds sprout, remove the bag.*

2. *Alternatively, snip 3-inch shoots from miniature tomato plants, set them 1½ inches deep in a 5-inch pot of moist mix, and cover with a plastic bag. Place in bright indirect light until roots form, in 10 days or so. Remove the bag.*

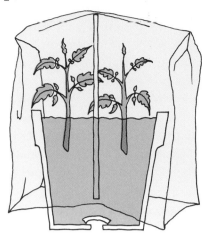

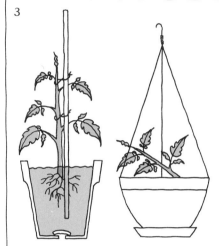

3. *Around October 10, transplant the most vigorous young plant to a 5-inch pot or hanging basket. Tie a pot-grown plant to a stake. In a basket, position the plant at a 45° angle. Water thoroughly. After two days of indirect light, move the plant to a sunny window.*

4. *Since tomatoes grown indoors require 10 to 12 hours of direct light daily to flourish, place a 100-watt incandescent bulb 15 inches above the plant to lengthen and brighten the short days of winter. In cloudy weather leave it on from 8 a.m. until 6 or 8 p.m.*

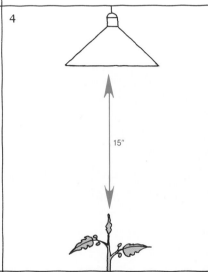

15"

5. *Starting 10 days after the plant has been potted, fertilize it once a week, using one level teaspoon of 20-20-20 fertilizer dissolved in a quart of water. If insects attack, take the plant outdoors briefly and spray with the appropriate insecticide. Follow label directions carefully and hold the nozzle 12 inches from the plant.*

6. *When flowers form, shake the plant gently each day to ensure pollination and fruit formation. If no buds appear by late November, pinch the tips off a few shoots to encourage budding.*

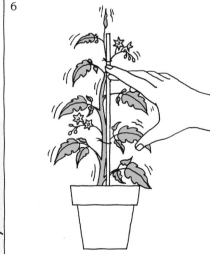

nutrients for most plants in your salad garden. Give these plants lots of sun, supplement sunlight with artificial light in winter, and never allow their soil to dry out.

Tomatoes are the vegetables you will want to try first, and Tiny Tim is a prolific producer. On a plant less than 12 inches high it bears as many as 200 fruits, each less than an inch in diameter. The tomatoes resemble clusters of grapes—even to having a rather sweet taste. Perfect companions in the salad bowl are Tom Thumb lettuce, a whole head of which is about the size of a baseball, and Baby cucumber, three to four inches long and borne on little vines. Keep the lettuce as cool as possible in summer, and feed it monthly with fish-emulsion fertilizer, which is high in leaf-stimulating nitrogen, rather than the bone meal or cottonseed meal that is applied to the fruiting vegetables.

With a vegetable patch in your kitchen, you may as well have a citrus grove in your living room. The soil mixture and size of pot for a dwarf citrus tree will be the same as for your midget vegetables, but with the amount of peat moss doubled to insure the acidity citrus trees need. In the case of something like a ponderosa lemon, flowering and fruiting in a 6-inch pot is quite a feat: on a tree that is not much more than a foot in height the ponderosa puts forth intensely fragrant white blossoms followed by fruits that weigh more than a pound apiece. Citrus trees grow best with high humidity, so you should set them on trays of wet gravel placed in bright sunshine to remind them of their tropical provenance. Keep your dwarf citrus trees cut back, both to increase fruit production and to restrain any overzealous growth.

Now let us suppose you live in an apartment that is in the heart of a 200-unit high-rise building. None of your windows provide enough sunshine for a citrus or any other plant. Despair not: comparatively modest installations of artificial light will serve your miniatures and dwarfs quite nicely. One 30-watt ordinary fluorescent tube, for example, with a reflector two feet long, will meet the light needs of three or four dozen plants in two-inch pots placed six inches beneath the tube.

Where these lamps are the sole source of light for your plants, keep them on 12 to 16 hours a day. You may have to determine the correct amount through trial and error, judging by the plants' color and lush or lanky growth. You can then easily maintain this schedule with an inexpensive automatic timer. Fluorescent tubes subjected to extensive use will not last forever. After a year's use, they should be replaced, for their effectiveness diminishes and the conquest of darkness cannot be achieved with halfway measures.

Indoor vistas created with tiny plants

A dedicated New York City rosarian removes the fading blossoms in his rose garden each morning, then takes the elevator eight floors down to begin his weekday journey to the office. An Indiana wildflower enthusiast pauses to admire the delicate blooms in an alpine meadow each time she passes through her living room. Such flights of gardening fancy are everyday realities for those who grow dwarf and miniature plants indoors.

After mastering the culture of these Lilliputian cousins of larger plants, many growers develop an irresistible urge to design a botanical collage of miniatures. The delight of the tiny but perfectly detailed leaves and flowers is intensified when the plants are combined to simulate landscapes. And the captivating little gardens that result are as practical as they are charming.

Apartment dwellers can enjoy as much gardening satisfaction as any suburban homeowner when they fill sunny windows with collections of dwarfs and miniatures. Low-budget, time-short landscapers can easily manage formal gardens that are only two or three feet in length. Climate is no obstacle—deserts can flourish in Maine, tropical jungles in Minnesota.

The creators of indoor landscapes are not fettered by such long-standing traditions as those associated with the ancient Japanese art of bonsai. Appropriate scale is the only binding rule. Since plants that are true miniatures may be scarce or even unavailable, the architects of tiny landscapes are free to mix genetic miniatures with plants kept small by manipulating their care and those that are simply small by nature. Tropical and hardy plants can be combined with a clear conscience and they are often mingled with inanimate objects, both natural and man-made.

The approaches to indoor landscaping that are illustrated on the following pages diverge widely. Yet each small garden is an artistically and horticulturally valid way to use plants. All these landscapes are bits of indoor gardening whimsy made possible because miniature plants cut them down to manageable size.

A White Sprite miniature gloxinia blooms among sedums, pearlwort and holly tucked into niches carved in a lava-rock island that rests on a white bonsai tray.

Miniatures under glass

With miniature plants, any gardener can enjoy the excitement of having a greenhouse. These Mexican glass cases, less than a foot wide, can, just as capably as their full-sized counterparts, give a temperamental little fern the humidity it craves or coax out-of-season flowers from a tiny gloxinia. Ventilation is regulated with a flick of the wrist, and as the sun changes with the seasons, these portables can move on to a brighter window sill.

Tsussima-holly, bird's-nest and Victorian brake ferns (top center) share the humidity in this glass castle with miniature African violets (top corners) and figs (lower corners). Plants stay in the inch-wide handmade pots for about two years.

A raised trough and a hanging pot filled with tiny ferns give depth to a miniature patio scene. A standard-sized fuchsia, kept root-bound in a 1-inch pot, is trained to simulate a tree (right). The clay brick path leads past a miniature African violet.

A woodland walk under lights

Designed to suggest the scenery along a woodland path, this 8-foot light garden holds a mélange of foliage, flowering and succulent plants whose original habitats were in both temperate and tropical climates. Though few of the plants are true forest natives, the garden nevertheless achieves its desired effect. One reason is the careful attention given to scale. Another is the selective grouping of plants so colors and textures of leaves and flowers blend harmoniously from one section of the garden to another. Since the plants vary in the kind and amount of care they require, they are kept in separate pots, surrounded and hidden by sphagnum moss.

The meticulous attention paid to realistic scale in the woodland walk above is clearly evident in this close-up from the left corner, where a life-sized carving of a white-breasted nuthatch provides a gauge of the garden's actual dimensions. Some of the plants, like the lavender and pale violet Cape primroses on the right side of the garden, are true miniatures, while others, such as the pink lady's-slipper orchid on the left side, are naturally small. Still others, like the ferns in the close-up, are kept small by shearing or root binding.

Dish-garden nature studies

Though the tiny gardens here and on the following pages look as though they were scooped up on nature hikes, all but one (the cluster of alpine geraniums on page 44) contain plants that would not grow side by side outdoors. Their designers have artfully combined tender and hardy plants, requiring only that they be compatible in scale and care. The results are intimate little suggestions of larger landscapes rather than slavish reproductions.

A Pixie Blue miniature African violet blooms beneath a canopy of rabbit's-foot fern. The dual-level pot was sculpted and planted to represent a miniature forest floor. Pearlwort growing at the base visually melds the pot with its 6-inch saucer.

Clumps of papyrus in a tiny pond shelter a pair of ceramic cranes. The glazed interior of the 5-inch bowl holds layers of charcoal and soil that anchor plant roots. Sand and gravel weigh down the soil to keep the water from becoming murky.

Four varieties of alpine geranium spring daintily from soil pockets cut into a piece of lava rock in this miniature landscape.

This simple 10-inch garden combines bead plant with miniature Boston ferns and rocks to set a woodland theme.

White-streaked rocks, vacation souvenirs, inspired this tiny desert garden planted in a white bonsai tray. The pigmy Joshua

trees and the giant's watch chain flanking the rocks require clipping to keep them in scale with the other small succulents.

Making the most of the small outdoors 3

Almost everyone who has gardened conventionally in spaces that are rather cramped has had fantasies about what he would do if given a large estate with broad vistas, towering trees and sweeping lawns. But outdoor gardening on a miniature scale can, to a surprising degree, satisfy such fancies, and the rewards go far beyond the fascination of perfection in tiny flowers, leaves and fruits. In a small area, individual beds can be prepared to accommodate miniatures and dwarfs that have vastly different soil requirements, from the dry alkalinity of the desert to the damp acidity of the forest floor. With miniature plants, it is possible to have both a rose garden and an alpine meadow, say, within touching distance of each other.

When gardening is done in spaces measured in only a few square feet, cultivation is so intensive that care is virtually continuous. Plants with tiny root structures may require watering twice a day; weeds must be pulled before they tower over the star attractions, and the gardener must be ever on guard against even a minor assault by pests or diseases.

An informal, flower-filled English garden in microcosm, such as one that Alice might have romped through on the other side of the looking glass, can be planted in any small space that receives five or six hours of sunlight a day. Miniature crane's-bill geraniums, for example, will begin to flower in spring and continue into summer, providing tiny pink blooms on plants that grow three to six inches tall. Despite their delicate appearance, these are hardy perennials and can remain in the garden through the worst of northern winters. Tiny pinks scattered through such an informal garden provide a summer-long display of flowers that both look and smell like scaled-down carnations.

But while the geranium will grow well in almost any garden soil, the pink is more particular. This miniature is an alpine plant—one that originated in the mountains above the tree line. Through

A harvest of full-grown miniature vegetables, including lettuce, cucumbers, red and yellow tomatoes and eggplants, rests appetizingly on a small dinner plate. Sharing the table is a standard-sized tomato.

49

many generations on the cold, bright, windy mountain tops, such plants have adapted themselves to short growing seasons and gravelly underpinnings by remaining small. Another alpine plant, the saxifrage, is so adept at clinging to rocky hillsides that its name means rock-breaker; the hornrim saxifrage, for example, is a 3-inch-tall miniature with ground-hugging silvery leaves and clusters of tiny white flowers borne on black stems.

Like the cacti of the Western deserts, top-of-the-mountain plants are not easy to grow where the soil is as naturally acidic as it is along the East Coast and in the Pacific Northwest. These plants prefer a soil that is neutral to slightly alkaline. To satisfy this need, it may be necessary for you to modify the chemistry of the soil in your alpine garden.

CHEMICAL ADJUSTMENTS The acidity or alkalinity of soil is generally related to its origin. In moist areas over rocks that contain only small amounts of calcium and magnesium, soils that developed from eroding rocks and the acidic humus of the forest floor usually remain acidic. Where the annual rainfall is scant and the bedrock is limestone, the soil tends to be alkaline.

A good starting soil for an alpine garden, one that satisfies the plants' need for good drainage, consists of one part topsoil, two parts sand and one part humus or peat moss. When this mix has been prepared in the planting bed, you can test its chemical balance with a home test kit or send soil samples to your local agricultural extension service for testing. The results will be indicated on a pH scale in numbers from 0 to 14. All you need to remember is that 7, the center of the scale, is neutral and that lower numbers indicate acidity, higher ones alkalinity.

For most alpine plants you would seek a pH rating of 7.0 to perhaps 7.5, but if instead your miniature garden is to consist of acid-loving plants like rhododendrons or camellias, you would strive for an acid pH of 5.0 to 5.5.

It is entirely feasible to change the existing acidity or alkalinity of your soil, especially for a small bed of miniatures. If you want to raise a low, acid pH by one point on the scale, simply rake in five pounds of ground limestone per 100 square feet—a bed that is 10 feet wide on each side. But if, instead, you want to reduce a high, alkaline pH by one point, add three pounds of iron sulfate or a half-pound of ground sulfur per 100 square feet.

AND DOUBLE CHECK It must be noted that these formulas are not foolproof. For example, heavy clay soil requires twice as much lime to achieve a given pH change as does sandy soil. To be certain that you have reached your goal, retest the treated soil after the chemical has had several months to do its job. You can expect that additional chemicals will be needed on the bed about every three years.

If your horticultural interests lead you to develop a bed of miniature cacti, your soil chemistry goals will be identical to those of alpine plants, but you will find the need for quick drainage even more important. This is especially true in regions with damp winters or very wet summers because the small and shallow root structures of these slow-growing plants are easily damaged. To achieve good drainage, add an extra measure of sand to the planting mix, making it one part soil, three parts sand and one part humus or leaf mold, plus half a cup of slow-acting bone-meal fertilizer per gallon of mix. Beneath this soil mix you need a six-inch layer of rocks, broken bricks, masonry chunks or gravel; masonry rubble and limestone are especially good because they both help to make the bed alkaline. If your land is distressingly flat, you may want to construct a mound or a slope; an angle of an inch or so per foot is enough to aid drainage and be visually attractive. Anything more precipitous may invite disaster in the form of landslides or washouts.

A cactus bed requires less watering than do most beds of miniatures—once a week in dry weather should be sufficient. You can test the soil for dryness with a finger; do not water unless the soil feels dry two or three inches down. But while less water is needed, much more fertilizing is required if you want to stimulate a cactus to bloom. In rainy areas, apply a phosphorus-rich fertilizer such as 15-30-15 once a month from April through July, mixing one tablespoon per gallon of water and applying the solution freely. Do not fret about the possibility of stimulating a surge of unwanted growth. Miniature cacti, especially such ball types as mammilaria and notocactus, grow very, very slowly even in the most favorable of environments. But stop fertilizing in midsummer; anything that stimulates new growth in August or later will increase the risk of damage from winter cold.

A well-drained cactus bed provides a compatible home for a number of other miniatures. Succulents such as the tiny living stones from South Africa and Bolivia do well there. Cresses can be planted to provide spreading mats of intense blue-green foliage: rock cress stays under four inches in height and produces white flowers in May, while stone cress sends forth pink flowers about a month later. If you like, you can also mix in a number of alpine perennials, such as a variety of baby's breath that grows only one inch high or a tricolored viola that is only two inches tall, called heart's ease. The latter is reputed to have been, appropriately enough, the favorite flower of Henry the Eighth.

CARING FOR CACTI

Elements of a formal design

A miniature formal garden offers all the beauty of its larger counterpart, for only a fraction of the trouble. Its geometric design can duplicate that of a famous garden, such as the parterre gardens at Williamsburg, or take on a shape all its own, as intricate as an Elizabethan knot garden or as simple as a diamond set in a square. At left are several suggested designs for a 4-by-4-foot garden, although each can be adapted to a larger or smaller site. When designing your formal garden, sketch the plan first on paper, letting one inch represent one foot of ground. Weave into your design one or all of the categories described below.

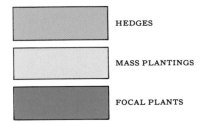

HEDGES

MASS PLANTINGS

FOCAL PLANTS

LIVING LINES OF HEDGES
A low, dense hedge, neatly sheared, creates unity and continuity in a formal garden design. A hedge may be used to frame a miniature garden or to form its internal lines. Dwarf boxwood is a good choice for a miniature hedge because of its slow growth, small evergreen leaves and the ease with which it can be pruned and shaped. Edging herbs like germander can also be used.

COLORING WITH MASS PLANTINGS
The open spaces of a formal miniature garden are usually filled with mass plantings of flowering bulbs, annuals or perennials. To keep the viewer's eye focused on the section's overall shape rather than on individual plants within it, use only one species and color of plant in each grouping. The plantings should balance each other within the design; if the north quadrant contains miniature red begonias, so should the south quadrant. Open spaces in a formal miniature garden can also be filled with a small-leaved ground cover, such as thyme or sedum, or with a wood-chip or pebble mulch.

BRINGING A GARDEN INTO FOCUS
A formal garden design contains at least one focal point, which attracts attention by its shape, color, size, texture or sound. A focal point may be a single specimen plant, such as a highly attractive ornamental tree or flowering shrub, or a group of plants with dark-hued, eye-catching flowers. A focal point may also be a man-made object, such as a fountain, birdbath, sundial or statue. If the focal point consists of flowers, provide an alternate focal point when the flowers are not in bloom. For a permanent focal point, such as an ornamental tree, choose a specimen that has several striking characteristics—spring flowers, vibrant foliage, shaggy bark—so it will continue to be attractive throughout the year.

Miniature roses, familiar to many gardeners as house plants *(page 32),* are by no means excluded from their outdoor place in the sun. They are very hardy, surviving winters to -30°, and they bloom almost continuously from May until frost. The flowers, usually a bit larger than a man's thumbnail, come in the full range of rose colors— white to pink, red, yellow, orange and even purple. The miniature bushes grow four to 18 inches tall and are often used to edge beds and borders of larger plants. They create a more dramatic effect when given a bed of their own, however, and they benefit greatly from being kept away from the competition of larger plants, which deprive them of light and water, and even from smaller rivals that are aggressive.

In a bed of miniature roses you may want to sample the entire range of sizes, beginning with the tiny Littlest Angel, which bears bright yellow flowers half an inch across on plants four inches tall. The middle-sized miniatures are the floribunda types that have the longest blooming season and produce dense clusters of tiny flowers. Tallest are the climbers that may grow five feet up but continue to bear miniature flowers.

The best soil mix for miniature roses is slightly acid, pH 6.0 to 7.0, which is usually easy to achieve if it does not exist naturally. The plants do have one absolute requirement: the roots must never be allowed to dry out. This means the planting mix must include abundant organic matter or be amended with humus or peat moss until it will hold sufficient water through dry spells. The addition of sand helps too, in keeping water from standing around the roots during wet weather. A good formula for the rose bed calls for one part garden loam, two parts humus or peat moss, and one part sand. Another way to retain moisture in the soil is to mulch around each plant with wood chips, uncut sphagnum moss, gravel, pine needles or chunky peat moss; this also keeps mud (and disease organisms) from splashing on the foliage. But even with such precautions, it is likely that you will need to water miniature roses twice a day during hot or windy weather.

Both root growth and flower production will be stimulated by the application of a fertilizer that is high in phosphorus. It should be used in spring, just before the leaf buds begin to open. One excellent source of phosphorus is bone meal, which can be dusted on the ground around each plant. This slow-acting organic fertilizer is safe to use; it will not burn the tiny, delicate roots that lie close to the surface of the soil.

Every ten days or so during the growing season, your tiny rose bushes need to be sprayed to guard them against pests and diseases,

A MOIST BED OF ROSES

53

especially the latter. Once you see evidence of a fungus or virus attack—blackened or yellowed leaves—there is not much you can do to halt its ravages. Removing faded flowers frequently will help prevent botrytis disease from taking hold. The only other care the roses are likely to need is a judicious pruning in early spring, with each cut made just above a swelling bud.

ACID-LOVING EVERGREENS   The dwarf forms of broad-leaved evergreens and needled conifers share the predilection of roses for acid soil, only more so. Most will grow well with a pH of 5.5 to 6.5, and a few, notably the rhododendrons, will do even better with a pH of 5.0 to 5.5. (The pH rating is logarithmic; a rating of 6.0 is ten times more acid than one of 7.0, but a rating of 5.0 is 100 times more acid than 7.0.) To satisfy this appetite for acid soil, stuff the evergreen bed with peat moss or acid compost—at least three or four parts for one part of garden loam and one part of sand. You can lower the pH further, if necessary, by watering around the bases of your tiny plants, using one tablespoon of aluminum sulfate dissolved in each quart of water. A mulch of pine needles or oak leaves continues the acidifying process. With properly prepared soil and an acidic mulch, the fertilizer needs of miniature evergreens are negligible; an annual light dusting with cottonseed meal is sufficient.

In fact, if you overfertilize, you may find yourself with a 6- or 8-foot dwarf conifer overshadowing your miniature garden. They shoot up surprisingly fast sometimes. If that happens, there is no remedy but to remove the impertinent plant.

There are true miniatures among the small evergreens. The tennis-ball cypress, a conifer that forms a perfect ball of dark green leaves about six inches in diameter atop a tiny trunk a few inches high, grows at a rate of one fourth to one half inch a year. It is unlikely to outgrow your miniature garden in this century. Less formal looking, and indeed rather serpentine, is the 10-inch-tall Japanese juniper. Planted in a border, its bluish foliage swirls in patterns reminiscent of the mosaic sidewalks of Rio de Janeiro.

A BONUS OF FLOWERS   Broad-leaved evergreen miniatures planted among such conifers provide a contrast in texture with their shiny leaves, and many of them add a floral display as well. The bog rosemary brings pink clusters of bloom into the miniature garden on bushes that are less than six inches tall, in shady places as well as sunny. Dwarf flowering flax is highly esteemed in England not only for its bell-like yellow or white flowers but for the ease with which it flowers in any sunny, well-drained soil, including Zones 4-8 of North America. Several species of rhododendrons are available in true miniature form, less than one foot tall. The Impeditum, which blooms in early spring, bears tiny clusters of royal purple flowers and is widely available. The Mayflower, a heavy bearer of pink flowers, is less common but by no means a rarity; it is often listed in the catalogues of rock-garden suppliers.

Evergreen gardens, like others based on miniatures, are subject to such close inspection that they need to be kept immaculate at all times. They must be kept scrupulously weeded; their beauty can be quickly obliterated by full-sized weeds. Also, if the dwarf conifers become scraggly, they should be pinched back even if you are reluctant to reduce their already diminutive size. Similarly, the spring-flowering evergreen shrubs should have their spent flowers removed as soon as they fade, and any dead stems should be cut back at the same time.

Miniature plants also adapt beautifully to another outdoor possibility: free-standing trough or sink gardens. If you do not happen to have an old stone watering trough languishing in the backyard, you can build your own, using a mixture of 1½ parts dry peat moss, 1½ parts perlite or vermiculite and 1 part portland cement, plus enough water so the mix will pour easily into a form made with two cardboard boxes, one inside the other. Planters made from this mixture will withstand winter temperatures down to -20°

TROUGH GARDENS

PLANNED INFORMALITY

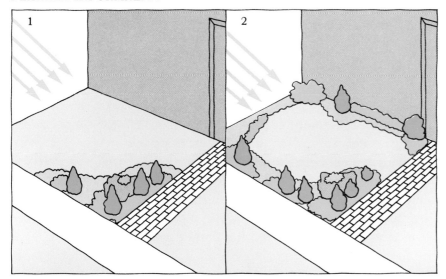

An informal miniature garden can be the focal point of a larger garden area (1) or it can fill the area completely (2). In either case, it must be carefully designed so sunlight reaches all the plants. Place larger plants on the garden's northern edge *to keep them from casting an afternoon shadow over the smaller plants. Inward curves are natural focal points for attractive trees or shrubs. Softly curving inner borders create a sense of motion, while a few roughhewn rocks add depth and dimension.*

without cracking, and are also light enough that a container 22 by 22 inches by 8 inches deep may be lifted without difficulty. You can style a sedate box for a formal rose garden or, depending on the mold you use, you can create a free-form planter that resembles natural rock and lends itself to a mountain or desert motif.

TINY TABLE TREATS   Should you want more than esthetic nourishment from your miniature garden, you can be at least slightly utilitarian as you satisfy your gourmet tastes and create conversation pieces for your dinner table by growing miniature vegetables. Most of these—corn, eggplants, tomatoes, cucumbers and pumpkins, for example—need full sun to prosper, but you might have reasonable success growing miniature lettuce in medium to light shade.

Like roses, most of these vegetables prefer slightly acid soil, with a pH of 6.0 to 7.0. If you spade peat moss and sand into your garden loam, seeking a mixture of approximately one third of each in the top six inches of the bed, you should achieve a good growing medium for vegetables.

Since your dainty tasty tidbits will be growing in such a restricted area, perhaps only 10 feet square, you will not want to risk losing any of your produce to marauding rabbits. Fencing the little plot is a worthwhile investment, and the fence will provide an additional bonus of clinging space for such upwardly mobile plants as cucumbers and tomatoes.

In any miniature garden that is replanted year after year, the nutrients near the surface need to be replenished periodically. A good way to rejuvenate a small vegetable patch is to spade in dried, odorless manure when the soil is prepared—a 50-pound bag evenly spread over the surface should be sufficient for a bed 10 feet square. Should some of the vegetables need further stimulus in midsummer, a solution of fish emulsion provides the needed lift without endangering the delicate plants. But be cautious; overfeeding is more hazardous to a miniature than underfeeding.

THE WATER WATCH   Care of miniature vegetables parallels that of their larger counterparts, although more frequent watering will be needed. The soil must not be allowed to dry out. Midday wilting of a plant's leaves is your signal to get out the hose; there is no margin for error with root structures so tiny.

Keep a sharp watch for signs of pest or disease attacks, and spray or dust selectively with a pesticide or fungicide designed to cope with your specific problem. Follow label directions carefully, especially warnings that specify the last day that it is safe to treat a vegetable before the harvest.

Sweet corn, one of the best liked of all vegetables, earns its keep in a garden of miniatures. Golden Midget, for example, will give you two ears, each six inches long, on a stalk that attains three feet in height in only two months. You must give corn enough space to prosper; maintain two feet between rows and six inches between plants so that breezes can do their essential cross-pollinating job. You may prefer to grow the White Midget variety; there are gardeners who swear that it is far sweeter than yellow corn. If you live in the lower half of the United States, where there is a long growing season, you should be able to harvest two successive two-month corn crops each season.

This bountiful productivity applies as well to other early-maturing vegetables. A slicing cucumber named Mini, for example, will produce four-inch fruits on two-foot bushes in only 55 days; three crops may be possible in regions where spring comes early and summer lingers late.

Some of these miniature vegetables, such as Tiny Tim tomatoes, can be grown successfully as house plants *(page 34),* but you are not likely to try growing watermelons or cantaloupes indoors. Small though their fruits may be, the vines flop around for a yard or so from the hills where the seeds are planted. Even in the outdoor garden, you will need to consider whether you can afford the space that melons will demand.

Probably the most efficient vegetable for your miniature garden is also the most exotic. It is the snow pea that you so often encounter, pod and all, in Chinese restaurants. Dwarf snow peas such as the Snowbird or the Little Sweetie variety, take up almost no space in the miniature vegetable garden when grown next to a fence. As they grow through the spring they require heavy watering, but you can enjoy their lovely white or purple flowers, much like those of ornamental sweet peas. They must be planted and harvested while the weather is still cool, and they are ready for harvesting in 60 days or less. The vines, less than two feet tall, will be gone by the beginning of summer, making space for the miniature tomato plants that you have started indoors.

Since it is the delicate shell and not the pea inside that delights the palate, snow peas are picked and eaten just as the peas inside the pod are starting to swell. After your harvest, perhaps you will treat your friends to the marvelous taste of *chao-hsüeh-tou*—fresh snow peas stir-fried with thinly sliced beef and canned bamboo shoots. Many gourmet cooks have tried to make this treat with defrosted frozen snow peas, but these do not have the crisp, delightful flavor of fresh peas that you picked only moments earlier from your very own garden of miniature vegetables.

GOURMET SPECIAL

57

Grand designs for little landscapes

Miniature outdoor gardens, originally planted in old stone sinks and horse troughs, became popular in England during the 1930s. Consisting mainly of alpine plants and low-growing rock plants, each tiny landscape was designed to evoke visions of a grander scene, perhaps a wild woodland or water garden, or a formal herb or rose garden.

A miniature garden serves the same delightful purpose today. Grown in movable containers or on a small patch of earth, it permits the creation of an elaborate landscape—complete with trees, hedges, flowers, lawns, paths and pools—in even the smallest of yards.

Scale is the most important design element of a miniature garden. The plants, when full grown, should appear to be the correct size in proportion to one another and to such accessories as walls, sundials and arbors. A dwarf evergreen tree should tower over a miniature rose bush; a tiny vine should have leaves smaller than the bricks in the small-scale wall it is meant to cover. Often, the size of the garden's site or container will determine its scale. A miniature garden the size of a chessboard will naturally require smaller trees, shrubs and flowers than one spread out over 100 square feet.

Containers vary widely, from a round birdbath to a long, narrow wooden box. Although picturesque stone sinks and troughs are now hard to find, modern imitations can be fashioned by hand from lightweight concrete or wood *(pages 60-61)*. The container should be strong and weather-resistant and have good drainage. It should also be in scale and harmony with the garden it holds.

Most outdoor miniature gardens, especially those containing hardy alpine and rock plants, require protection during winter. After the ground has frozen, mulch the garden with a light covering of hay or pine needles. If the garden is in a portable container, set it in an out-of-the-way corner or cold frame, sheltered from drying winds and direct sun. Water the plants sparingly when the soil is dry. Once spring approaches, remove the winter mulch, increase watering and move the garden, if it is portable, back to a place where its dainty, irresistible beauty can be viewed to best advantage.

A miniature garden mimics itself with a display of even tinier trough gardens. Drought-resistant succulents are planted in the troughs, which dry out quickly.

Well-contained gardens

Plants that are culturally compatible are needed for a container-grown miniature garden, often called a sink garden. Bog-dwelling plants, which thrive in moist, acid soil, can be grown in one container; alpine plants, which prefer porous, alkaline soil, in another. Several large rocks, positioned with discrimination, are more effective than many small ones. Trailing plants draped over the rim of the container help blend it with the tiny landscape it supports.

Several sink gardens, brimming with a variety of miniature plants, rest snugly on large moss-covered stones. Made from a lightweight mixture of portland cement, peat moss and perlite, the containers are moved to a nearby terrace when the plants are in bloom. In winter, they are stored in a cold frame. Many of the plants are saxifrages, an enormous group of small plants, all of which thrive in rocky limestone soil.

The alpine plants of this miniature rock garden are tucked among chunks of tufa, a porous limestone that absorbs water easily. The daisy-like plant at the tip of the tiny trowel is a Bellium minutum; the twiggy shrub above it is a dwarf azalea. At top center is a miniature jade tree.

A small pool, made from a copper pan painted black, is the focal point of this miniature woodland garden. Plants include a dwarf sawara false cypress (bottom center) and a dwarf Canadian hemlock (top right). A small branch has been laid across the water to simulate a fallen log.

A mountain in the yard

A mountainscape is one of the most dramatic of all designs for an outdoor miniature garden. It should look as if it were carved by a glacier. Make it slope north or northwest so it will get some summer sun but not so much that the soil dries out each day. Slant the rocks slightly inward and downward to encourage water to flow in among the miniature alpine or rock plants. Some of the plants in the Seattle mountainscape below are shown life-sized on pages 64 and 65.

The stark, cool beauty of a jagged mountainside is reflected in microcosm in this miniature alpine garden. Constructed from blue slate, it incorporates a recirculating pool. The ridge of trees in the background includes dwarfed hemlocks and alpine firs.

Mountain plants, life-sized

VERONICA BIDWILLII: *This New Zealand shrub bears its flowers above thick, leathery foliage.*

RAOULIA LUTESCENS *(top)* and HYPERICUM YAKUSIMANA: *Both serve as tiny flowering ground covers.*

RHODODENDRON PUMILUM: *This 5-inch-tall shrub forms dense rosettes that bloom in spring.*

ERODIUM CHAMAEDRYOIDES ROSEUM: *Only 3 inches tall, this is a tiny member of the geranium family.*

VACCINUM VITIS-IDAEA MINUS: *Stems with evergreen leaves creep along the ground at a height of 4 inches.*

POLYTRICHUM COMMUNE: *It spreads quickly to form a low mat of starlike foliage.*

DRABA SIBIRICA: *Succulent leaves of this Siberian native form ¼-inch rosettes that bear yellow flowers in spring.*

DRABA BRYOIDES IMBRICATA: *This alpine plant grows in a round dense cushion shape that protects it from strong mountain winds.*

The ancient art of bonsai 4

The word in Japanese literally means "to cultivate in a tray," but bonsai implies much more. When wrought by a master, a bonsai is as spare and evocative as a haiku poem, conveying the spirit of ancient trees, survivors isolated in a field or clinging tenaciously to a cliff, whose gnarled branches yet reach upward toward the light.

Unlike most other art forms, the creation of a bonsai is a continuous event. Bonsai trees 200 years old are not uncommon in Japan, and one miniature bonsai no taller than your thumb recently passed its 80th birthday in Kyoto. Obviously, only carefully tended plants could live so long, and it is this need for constant attention that makes bonsai such a demanding art.

The major factor in the control of bonsai growth is pruning—not just of the branches but, even more important, of the roots. Even after the tree has reached its designated size and shape, it is periodically unpotted, root-pruned and repotted with new soil. Thus, the plant stays the same size and remains healthy.

In addition to the pruning ritual, the bonsai requires daily ministrations, primarily watering. As noted in Chapter 2, the small amount of soil in a miniature pot dries out quickly, and one hot, waterless day could kill a plant upon which you have lavished years of care. *Mame* (pronounced mah-may) bonsai, miniatures of miniatures less than seven inches tall, are especially vulnerable—leading a successful Japanese comedian, according to reliable reports, to hurry home several times a day between appearances to meet the watering schedule of his collection of 1,000 *mame* bonsai.

In Japan, where extremely low temperatures are rare, bonsai has traditionally been practiced on hardy trees such as pines, junipers and maples that stay outdoors all year long; indeed, they need a period of dormancy in the winter cold, and exposure to the elements helps keep them small. But an American innovation extends bonsai techniques to the indoor cultivation of tropical plants,

Foemina junipers, with upper bark peeled to simulate great age, create a bonsai forest 4 feet tall. Each tree in this arrangement, nicknamed "God's Protector," represents one of the owner's grandchildren.

Five familiar bonsai styles

Trees trained as bonsai, like trees in nature, take on many shapes. Five common bonsai styles are illustrated below—each in its three different forms. Let the tree you select suggest its own style. Remember that an asymmetrical tree is usually more interesting than one with matching left and right sides. To balance the asymmetry, set the tree off-center in its pot.

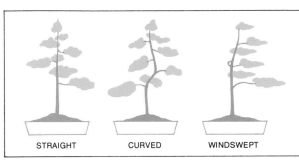

STRAIGHT   CURVED   WINDSWEPT

UPRIGHT

In the Upright style of bonsai, the lower third of the trunk is bare. Branches of the Straight and Curved Upright forms alternate from side to side, while in the Windswept form windward branches are pruned or bent toward the leeward side. Although the tip of an Upright tree lines up over its base, the tip of a Windswept form may lean slightly away from its base if the overall direction of the trunk is upright.

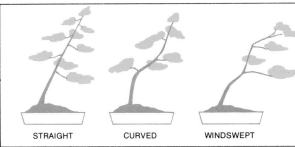

STRAIGHT   CURVED   WINDSWEPT

SLANTING

A tree trained in the Slanting style of bonsai is usually planted at an angle between 45° and 90°, and is set to one side of its container to balance its far-reaching tip. In the straight form, branches on the side to which the trunk leans are trained at a slightly wider angle than those on the opposite side. This creates an optical effect that keeps the tree from looking as if it is about to topple over.

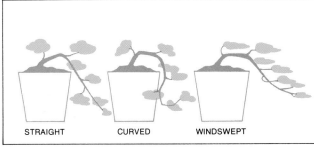

STRAIGHT   CURVED   WINDSWEPT

CASCADE

In the Cascade style of bonsai, a tree's tip descends below the base of its trunk and may also descend below the base of its pot. A deep container gives the tree a platform from which to flow. An easy way to train a cascading bonsai is first to grow a Slanting tree (above). After the lowest branch on the slanted side thickens sufficiently, the trunk is cut off above the branch, which forms a cascading trunk.

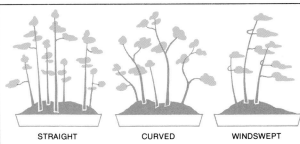

STRAIGHT   CURVED   WINDSWEPT

FOREST OR GROUP

A forest or Group style of bonsai is best accomplished with a collection of thin-trunked, sparsely branched trees of the same species. Trees with the best branches are positioned near the edge where they lean away from the others, as if to reach for light. Planting larger trees in front suggests a close-up forest view; kept in back, they create a distant view. Generally an odd number of trees is used.

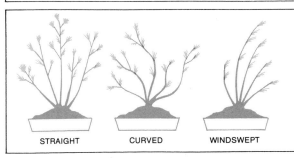

STRAIGHT   CURVED   WINDSWEPT

CLUMP

The Clump style is suitable for shrubs, but because the resilient wood of most shrubs tends to return to its original position after wiring, the Curved and Windswept forms are somewhat difficult to accomplish. For a Curved Clump, select a shrub with wood already twisted; for a Windswept Clump, prune the plant's windward branches. Avoid an unnaturally symmetrical and one-dimensional fan shape.

which have no marked dormancy period. This enables even those who live in harsher climes or in small apartments to grow bonsai. Woody-stemmed tropicals (the woody stem usually retains the shape you give it) such as ficus, podocarpus and pittosporum not only adapt well to bonsai training but have the further advantage of growing rapidly while young; the plants quickly reward you with visible progress. Other plants suitable for indoor bonsai, though more commonly grown outdoors, include the Kingsville dwarf boxwood and the ever-popular dwarf Japanese juniper.

A LOOK OF MATURITY

To translate the essence of a weathered, maturely serene tree into a small plant in a shallow tray requires more than a modicum of forethought. Before you begin pruning, pinching and wiring a plant to shape it, you must have an idea—a Platonic ideal, if you will—of what your living sculpture will eventually look like. From centuries of observing trees old and young, the Japanese have developed several means of shaping young trees to make them look mature in a pot. They noted that a tree trunk often grows away from a heavy limb, for example, as if the tree were trying to regain equilibrium. This natural phenomenon is reproduced in a bonsai by pruning so that heavier limbs grow from the outside of the curve of a trunk. From hundreds of similar observations, bonsai classifications have evolved. The five most common are the Upright, Slanting, Cascade, Group-planting and Clump styles (opposite page). These are not rigid forms; rather, they provide guidelines to help you work with any plant you choose.

The simplest is the Upright style. There are many variations. For example, the Straight Upright (also called Formal Upright in the United States because of a long-enduring mistranslation) takes the classic shape of an evergreen whose stately trunk draws a perpendicular line from earth to heaven. The Curved Upright (also called Informal Upright in this country) is essentially vertical but the trunk curves gracefully. In the Windswept Upright style, the branches are pruned or shaped to create the effect of a tree buffeted by incessant winds. Of these three common variations, Windswept is the most difficult to create.

AN ANGLE ON STYLE

Bonsai in the Slanting style represent trees that have been subjected to harsher forces. They may lean at any angle from a few degrees off the vertical on down, but are generally set at an angle somewhere between 45° and the upright position. Slanting-style bonsai set at a more acute angle may look ready to fall over.

Perhaps the most dramatic style in bonsai is the Cascade style; it is also one of the more difficult to work with. Unlike other styles, a cascading bonsai is planted in a deep pot to give it a stable and

Guides to beauty, balance

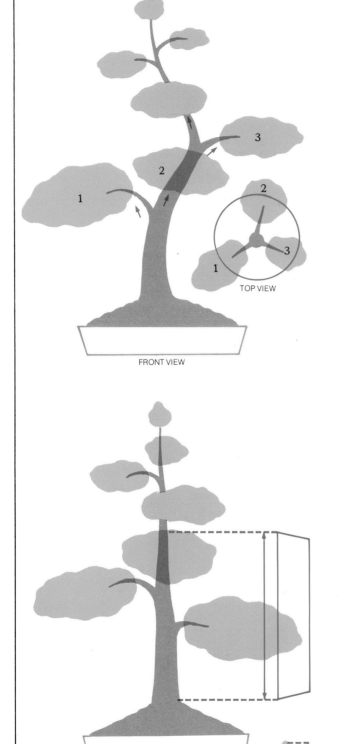

FRONT VIEW

TOP VIEW

FRONT

BACK

By studying the creation of a basic Upright bonsai tree, a novice can learn many of the guidelines that bonsai artists have followed for centuries. Begin with the selection of a plant. A good choice for a first effort is a hardy conifer such as a juniper. Find a healthy, vigorous young plant. Look for an interesting configuration, but remember that your efforts here are to bring out the unique character of any tree you choose. Select a container only after the tree is shaped.

SHAPING THE TREE

In shaping a bonsai, study the tree's traits, visualize the way it would look in the wild, then prune any obviously undesirable elements. The following suggestions for shaping an Upright bonsai are centuries old, but they are not strict rules; adapt them to suit your particular tree.

● *Select as the tree's front the side that reveals the best features of the trunk. If a trunk curves, display the curve to best advantage.*

● *Keep approximately the bottom third of the tree free of branches. This reveals the structure of the trunk, gives direction to your bonsai and creates the illusion of age. Choose as the lowest branch the longest and thickest one that reaches to the right or left of the front (1). Train it to reach slightly forward, as if the tree were welcoming the viewer (inset, above left).*

● *Select a back branch slightly higher up to give the bonsai depth (2), training it to the right or left (inset).*

● *To offset the first branch, choose a third one slightly higher, on the opposite side of the trunk (3).*

● *Once the first three branches are established, try to continue this pattern to create a spiral of higher and shorter branches, pruning if necessary to make them thinner and smaller. If the trunk is curved, be sure the heaviest branches emerge from the outer edge of the curve (arrows).*

SELECTING A CONTAINER

Once shaped, a tree must usually spend at least a year in a deeper training pot before it is planted in a bonsai pot. The selection of a permanent container is very important to the overall composition of your bonsai; some guidelines follow:

● *Let the shape of the pot reflect the style and character of the tree. A strong, rugged tree needs an equally rugged rectangular pot, while a delicate tree needs a more fragile-looking oval or round tray.*

● *Earth tones complement a quiet nonflowering tree, while brighter colors can enhance a showier plant.*

● *Generally, keep the length of the pot about two thirds the height of the tree (left), but if your tree is particularly delicate or massive, select a pot that will show the tree at its best.*

● *Match the depth of the pot and the height of the soil mound, if there is one, to the thickness of the tree's trunk at its base (left).*

● *For a very small or unusually shaped bonsai, select a pot that contributes about 40 per cent to the visual whole of the composition (inset, left).*

heightened platform from which to flow. This bonsai represents a tree growing on the edge of a precipice. It conveys the idea of two opposing forces: the downward pull of gravity and the upward thrust of light-seeking leaves and branches.

Assuming you want to train a mature plant—avoiding the several years' wait for a seedling to develop—there are two possible ways to find a suitable candidate for bonsai: collecting from the wild or buying from a nursery. Collecting is difficult. You need permission from the property owner or governmental authority to dig up a wild plant, and its chances of survival are slim. If you do find a wild specimen too good to pass up, the best time to transplant is in early spring. Dig as much of the root ball as possible, wrapping the roots with damp uncut sphagnum moss and wrapping the whole tree in burlap or sheet plastic. At home, plant the tree as quickly as possible in a large pot or planter box; water it thoroughly, prune the top to match the reduced root structure and leave it in this temporary container for at least a year, keeping the soil moist but not soggy. In some cases it may take two years for a wild plant to adjust to cramped quarters so it can be shaped.

Even a nursery plant—which already has a compact root ball and has been living in a pot—will rarely survive the radical pruning needed to put it immediately into a shallow bonsai pot. The move must be made in stages to ease the shock; usually the plant will move into an intermediate training pot after the first root pruning.

It takes practice to discern the eventual bonsai form in an untrained plant. Look not for the grotesque but for the provocative, and study the trunk rather than the foliage. If your bonsai is to conjure up the image of an ancient tree, the trunk should taper evenly from the base. A plant that has the same trunk thickness from its base to its upper branches will not appear to be old. Two ways to thicken a thin trunk are illustrated on pages 74 and 75. If natural gaps exist in the plant's branches, consider them a virtue. "A gap," says one bonsai expert, "is a decision that the tree has made for you, a space which you must incorporate into your design."

Once you have your diamond-in-the-rough safely home, select a cloudy, windless day to begin working on it; sun and wind will dry the plant too rapidly. Before liberating it from its initial container, decide on the style you want to create *(page 68)*. Consider how you will eventually shape it. Does it lend itself most readily to an Upright style? Or is it a shape that would only make a cascading bonsai? Bonsai are meant to be seen from all directions, but with a front view that presents the plant at its best, so you must decide where the front is. As one expert puts it, "It is the view that should lead you to

A TRAINING CONTAINER

exclaim, 'What a marvelous trunk!' If you are led to say, 'Look at all those leaves,' then you haven't found the front."

With the basic style decisions made, remove any branches you are sure you will not want. On a healthy tree, such cuts will leave light green and cream wounds. These are sometimes smeared with mud or a tree-wound dressing, but such treatment is not necessary. It is more important that you use clean pruning shears to avoid transmitting infection.

Soil for a bonsai, used in a training pot as well as in a shallow display tray, is notable in two ways: it is formulated to give the tree minimum nourishment while keeping it healthy, and it is sifted to separate it into different-sized particles for better aeration and drainage. You can buy premixed bonsai soil at some nurseries, or

The classic bonsai plants

Over the years, certain trees and shrubs have proved particularly amenable to the harsh discipline imposed by the art of bonsai. Listed here are 45 such plants; the zones *(map, page 151)* indicate the extremes of winter cold that each will tolerate.

*Outdoor bonsai that can be kept indoors in winter

EVERGREEN BONSAI

*LITTLELEAF BOXWOOD Zones 6-10
Buxus microphylla

TRUE CEDAR Zones 7-10
Cedrus species

FALSE CYPRESS Zones 5-8
Chamaecyparis species

*JAPANESE HOLLY Zones 5-10
Ilex crenata

SAN JOSE JUNIPER Zones 3-10
Juniperus chinensis San Jose

SHIMPAKI JUNIPER Zones 6-10
J. chinensis Shimpaki

JAPANESE JUNIPER Zones 3-10
J. squamata prostratra

DWARF ALBERTA SPRUCE Zones 1-9
Picea glauca albertiana

NORWAY SPRUCE Zones 1-9
P. abies

SCOTCH PINE Zones 1-9
P. sylvestris

JAPANESE BLACK PINE Zones 3-10
P. thunbergiana

*PODOCARPUS YEW Zones 8-10
Podocarpus macrophyllus maki

FIRE THORN Zones 4-10
Pyracantha species

AZALEA Zones 3-10
Rhododendron species

YEW Zones 3-9
Taxus species

DECIDUOUS BONSAI

TRIDENT MAPLE Zones 5-10
Acer buergeranum

JAPANESE MAPLE Zones 5-10
A. palmatum

RED MAPLE Zones 1-10
A. rubrum

SERVICEBERRY Zones 2-9
Amelanchier species

RED CHOKEBERRY Zones 4-10
Aronia arbutifolia

BARBERRY Zones 4-10
Berberis species

SIBERIAN PEA TREE Zones 2-9
Caragana arborescens

HORNBEAM Zones 3-9
Carpinus species

HACKBERRY Zones 4-7
Celtis species

FLOWERING QUINCE Zones 4-10
Chaenomeles species

COTONEASTER Zones 3-10
Cotoneaster species

HAWTHORN Zones 2-7
Crataegus species

BEECH Zones 3-9
Fagus species

GINKGO Zones 3-10
Ginkgo biloba

WINTERBERRY Zones 3-8
Ilex verticillata

LARCH Zones 1-9
Larix species

COMMON PRIVET Zones 4-9
Ligustrum vulgare

SWEET GUM Zones 5-10
Liquidambar styraciflua

CRAB APPLE Zones 2-9
Malus species

FLOWERING APRICOT Zones 7-10
Prunus mume

AZALEA Zones 3-8
Rhododendron species

SPIREA Zones 2-10
Spiraea species

BALD CYPRESS Zones 5-10
Taxodium distichum

ELM Zones 2-6
Ulmus species

WISTERIA Zones 5-9
Wisteria sinensis

JAPANESE ZELKOVA Zones 6-10
Zelkova serrata

INDOOR BONSAI

NATAL PLUM
Carissa grandiflora

WEEPING FIG
Ficus benjamina

COMMON GARDENIA
Gardenia jasminoides

COMMON OLIVE
Olea europaea

you can mix your own. Start by digging deep enough to reach clay soil beneath the humus-rich topsoil of your garden. You do not want a fertile soil. Bake the clay soil in the sun for a week. Then sieve it through a screen of hardware cloth with ¼-inch openings to remove stones and other debris. Sieve it again through finer screen with ⅛-inch openings to remove the finest particles. Discard the largest and smallest particles. What you have left is the clay ingredient of the basic bonsai soil mix. Fine particles are removed because they settle between larger particles and prevent the free flow of water and air. The other ingredients you need are aquarium gravel and a fibrous humus material such as peat moss, leaf mold or compost. Combine the three ingredients in equal parts, mixing thoroughly. Expert bonsai growers tailor the soil mix to suit each species that is grown.

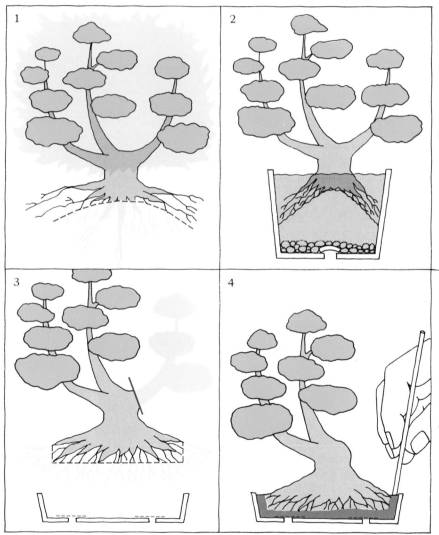

ROOT-PRUNING TECHNIQUES

1. *To start a bonsai, prune its roots in spring after shaping the top (page 70). Unpot the plant and gently free the soil. Keep the roots damp. Gather outer roots to one side; cut the central roots 1 inch below the base of the trunk (dotted line).*

2. *Cover the drainage hole of a training pot with a shard, add ½-inch of gravel, and fill with a mound of bonsai soil mix (page 72). Spread uncut roots over the mound and cover with soil. Place the pot in water until the surface is damp. Drain, set in shade for two weeks, then return to the sun.*

3. *The following spring, move the plant into a bonsai pot after further pruning. Place a piece of screen over each drainage hole. Add a thin layer of aquatic gravel and a mound of bonsai soil mix. Unpot the tree, free the roots as before, and trim them ½ inch smaller than the inside of the pot.*

4. *Set the tree in the pot, pour soil over the roots and twist the tree gently to settle the soil. Cover the roots with more soil, tamping around the edges. Set the pot in water, and keep out of direct sun. Water the base of the tree, gradually exposing the thickest roots.*

For a conifer, add an extra measure of sand; for an acid-loving plant such as a camellia, add an extra measure of humus.

If your nursery plant, after preliminary pruning, is ready to take up residence in its training pot, cover any drainage hole in the pot with a clay shard and line the bottom with a thin layer of gravel, then fill with the coarse-screened bonsai soil. The container is now ready for the plant.

THE FIRST ROOT PRUNING

Remove the plant from its nursery container and spread the roots out gently. You may have to cut away thick, winding roots to free the rest. Since a plant absorbs water and nutrients through the mesh of fine hairs near the growing tips of its roots, your ultimate goal is to create a small, shallow root system that consists primarily of these feeder roots rather than of long pipeline roots. Therefore, at this first stage, remove all roots directly under the base of the trunk, including the taproot if the plant has one. But leave a layer of roots around the top of the root ball *(page 73)*. Put the plant in its training pot, making sure the roots radiate evenly over a mound of bonsai potting mix. Water thoroughly. Do not apply any fertilizer for a month or two; it will injure the freshly pruned roots. Then fertilize once a month during the growing season, poking a few small holes in the soil and spooning in a slow-acting organic fertilizer such as cottonseed meal, bone meal or dried blood. The following spring, make sure the plant is vigorous and healthy; if it is not, postpone moving it to a bonsai pot.

Before shifting the plant from its training pot, you will want to shape it further. Ideally, branches should spiral up the tree in sets of

TAPERING A TRUNK

To make a pencil-thin bonsai trunk grow thicker and taper upward, so the miniature tree will look older, cut off the trunk above a branch where the tapering should begin (far left). Wire the branch (page 77) and gently bend it upward to create a new vertical leader for the tree. Position the branch so it will hide the cut when the trunk is viewed from the front. In subsequent years, repeat the procedure with another branch higher up the tree (left center).

three, without looking too precisely arranged *(page 70)*. The lowest branch will be the longest and widest, as it is in nature, while subsequent branches become thinner and shorter. An important word to remember is "ramification." The main branches of a good bonsai will be ramified—that is, divided again and again into smaller branches and twigs. This you accomplish by pinching back the tips. The lowest pair of branches should seem to reach out slightly as if to embrace the viewer, and a third branch at the rear of the plant gives the bonsai depth.

Triangular-shaped trees are among the easiest to work with; they can be trained to any bonsai style. The entire tree should form a scalene triangle—one having three sides of unequal lengths—if you connect the top of the tree with the tips of the lowest branches. The same should be true when you view it from the sides or the back. Any growth that extends beyond the edges of such imaginary triangles should be cut back. Try to form smaller triangles with each branch as you become adept at thinning, pinching and pruning. This technique keeps the tree small but healthy. Left on its own, the tree would grow upward and become thickest on top. Shaded by the top, lower branches would die. The triangle shape lets light reach all branches to keep them functioning.

Such guidelines will help you create a small, healthy tree that gives the impression that it has lived long, endured much and is now mellowed and serene. But each plant has its own growth pattern. The plant you select is not likely to match any given style perfectly. You are free to modify and adapt guidelines as you see fit. With

GUIDED BY TRIANGLES

SHAPING WITH PRUNING SHEARS
To create a thick, zigzagging trunk on a young bonsai tree, cut off the trunk just above a branch where you want the first bend to appear (far left). Use sharp pruning shears to ensure a clean cut. In subsequent years, make a second cut above a new branch pointing in the opposite direction (left center). In addition to creating zigzags in the trunk, the repeated cuttings slow the tree's growth and thus thicken the trunk. The same technique can be used to create angular branches.

practice, you will learn to prune and shape each plant to bring out the best in it, no matter what its shape.

When your plant is ready to be moved to a shallow bonsai pot, prune and repot in a single session as you did the first time. This is generally done in early spring except in the case of slow-growing pines. These produce new roots only in spring and early summer, and interfering with that process will destroy the trees. Instead, repot pines between August and March. The tools you will need are relatively few: sharp scissors for pruning small roots, pruning shears for thicker roots and limbs (the hook-and-blade rather than the anvil type), a sharp knife, a wire cutter and a chopstick or similar wooden stick. You will also need plastic or galvanized window screening to cover drainage holes (there is no room for the usual shards of broken crockery in a shallow bonsai pot), and copper wire in varying diameters for shaping trunks and branches. Such wire comes in gauges from 8 to 24, with 8 the largest size. A rule of thumb is that the wire should be about one third the diameter of the thickest section of the wood being shaped. Sizes thicker than 16, used for wiring trunks and heavy branches, must be annealed—heated and cooled to make them more flexible. You may be able to buy annealed wire, or you can treat it yourself by placing it over a grill until it is red hot, then letting it cool.

REFINING THE SHAPE   On a cloudy, windless day, with tools, shallow bonsai container and potting soil at hand, proceed with the definitive shaping. When you begin pruning, remember always to cut just above or beyond a node or a branching point, and leave buds that point in the direction you want growth to take; the thrust of growth will go immediately into lateral shoots just below a cut.

After the tree is pruned and shaped to your satisfaction, proceed with the root pruning. Unpot the plant, remove the soil, prune the roots to fit comfortably into the shallow bonsai pot *(page 73),* and repot as a true bonsai.

Again, line the pot with a thin layer of gravel, followed by the bonsai soil mix. Put in enough soil mix so the root ball will sit high enough for the crown of the plant to be even with or higher than the rim of the pot *(page 73)*. Place the tree in the pot. Avoid positioning the trunk in the exact center of the pot. Bonsai trees are not fashioned to grow symmetrically, nor would they do so in nature. Make a conscious effort to position the trunk so the tree looks balanced, with its heavier foliage extending over more of the pot. Add soil on top of the root ball and twist the tree gently to let the loose soil mix sift among the roots. Fill the container with more soil and, using the chopstick, work the soil down around the edges of the pot where there are no roots. Tap the container to settle the soil further. Use a brush to smooth the surface. Slope the soil somewhat below the rim of the pot to permit watering without an overflow.

Now set the pot in a basin of water almost to the rim, letting it soak until the top of the soil looks wet. Let it drain, and place it out of direct sunlight for at least a week. Move it by stages into sunlight, giving the plant a chance to adapt gradually. Now you are ready to shape the plant with wire if the styling calls for this technique.

Wiring is such a ticklish job that you may want to practice first on a branch from a garden tree. Put on the wire first, then bend only once, and only in one direction at one spot—bending a branch back and forth tears wood tissue and injures it.

Always start wiring at the lowest or thickest part of a trunk or branch and wire up or out. In wiring the trunk, anchor one end of the wire in the soil among the roots; in wiring branches, wrap the wire first around the trunk for leverage. The wire must be snug, but not so tight that it cuts into the plant, and it should spiral upward or outward in evenly spaced loops kept at a 45° angle *(below)*. If the bark of the tree is tender, wrap the wire first with tape. After all the wires are in place to start the shaping, apply gentle pressure to move branches into position. If a branch will not bend as far as you would

WIRE SCULPTURE

SHAPING WITH WIRE

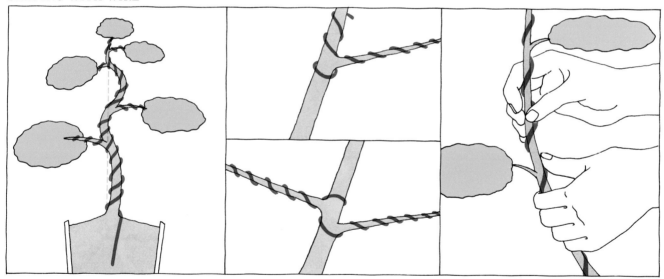

You can shape a young woody bonsai plant in spring after withholding water from it for a day. Anchor in the soil a piece of copper wire about ⅓ the diameter of the trunk. Wrap the wire around the trunk snugly at a 45° angle in bands ½ inch apart.

To wire a branch, secure a wire around the trunk, then wrap it under, over and along the branch (top). Avoid crushing leaves or twigs. Two branches can be wrapped with a single long wire (bottom). Begin at the trunk, wiring first one branch, then the other.

Using your thumbs as support, bend the trunk or branch gently into the shape you want. Bend in only one direction to avoid tearing wood tissues. Remove the wire in three to six months. Remove and rewire it sooner if it cuts into the bark of a fast-growing tree.

EASY BONSAI WITH A MUM

1. *Create a bonsai in less than a year with a rooted cutting of a special small chrysanthemum variety. In April, plant it over a mound of potting soil in a training pot. Over a few weeks, prune at every second or third node until only the two lowest leaves remain. Keep the strongest new shoot that sprouts from the leaf axils.*

2. *When the new shoot is 3 inches tall, unpot the plant, remove the soil with tepid water, snipping all but seven to nine of the biggest roots. Straddle the plant on a flat-bottomed rock and gently bind roots and rock with soft cotton cord.*

3. *Prepare a second pot and set the rock-bound plant in it, surrounded by a collar of window screen lined with newspaper. Fill the collar with soil, covering the roots; pack the soil firmly. Water thoroughly. Pinch the tip of the plant to encourage branching.*

4. *If you wish, shape the stem and branches with wire as they thicken (page 77). Do not wire over leaves or small branches. The fast-growing mum will need rewiring once or twice to prevent the wire from cutting the plant. Water from above, gradually exposing the roots to the sun.*

5. *By July, most of the rock should be exposed. Remove the collar and wire, pinch branches to thicken them, and turn the pot to promote even growth. When buds begin to show color, transplant the mum to a bonsai pot, in regular soil. Trim the underground roots into a shape slightly smaller than that of the bonsai pot (dotted line).*

6. *Ready to display by September, the mum should bloom for at least two months. Before the first frost, move it to an unheated garage until spring; water enough to prevent it from drying out. A bonsai mum will live for about 20 years.*

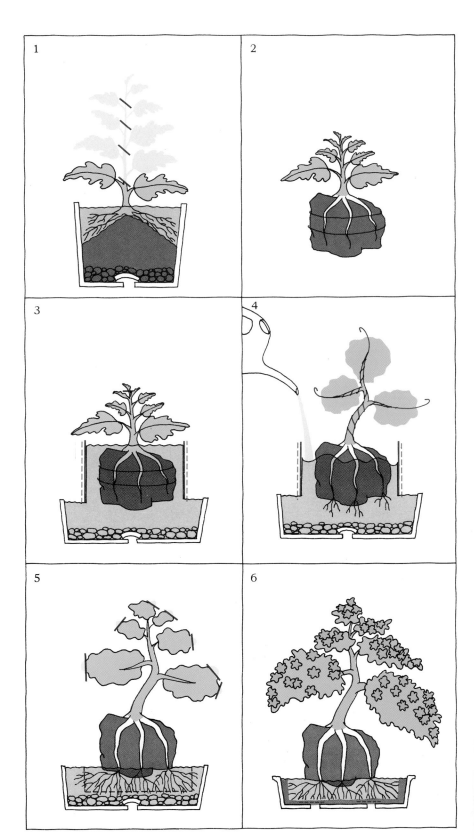

like, put on a second length of wire to provide even firmer support.

You now have a bonsai—which is to say, you have only just begun. The copper training wires may stay on for as long as one growing season, but with fast-growing plants you will need to rewire every few weeks so the wires do not make furrows in the trunk or branches. After allowing a month or two for the plant to recuperate, resume fertilizing once a month as before. If fertilizer salts or other undesirable deposits accumulate, dip the bonsai, pot and all, in water to wash it clean.

Trees should be repotted and root-pruned whenever they threaten to become pot bound. Old conifers need repotting every three to five years, deciduous trees every other year or even annually, and some young trees and fast-growing tropicals may need it two or three times a year. Each time you repot the plant, remove wedge-shaped sections of the central soil, alternating so that only part of the soil is taken away and replaced each time. Thus, the fine feeder roots you create by root pruning will continue to have fresh soil to feed upon.

PERPETUAL REPOTTING

As noted earlier, watering is your main concern. As a rule, a bonsai needs water once a day during the spring, two or three times a day during the summer, back to once a day in the fall, and perhaps once or twice a week in the winter. Check the soil often; whenever it is dry, water immediately. Do not worry about overwatering; the special soil mix you have provided will drain fast and prevent root rot, and you must supply the roots with fresh water regularly. If you go away for a few days, you can water the tree well, place it in a windless, shaded place, and expect it to survive. For longer absences, someone will have to come by to water the bonsai, or you will have to board it at a plant nursery or with a fellow bonsai devotee.

Generally, a bonsai needs the same light conditions that its full-sized counterpart does. However, hot summer sunlight may be too severe for even the toughest of them and should be filtered. Remember also to turn your bonsai periodically to keep it from becoming unbalanced with heavy growth on one side.

To achieve the necessary winter dormancy, hardy bonsai need cold temperatures—well under 50°. But they cannot endure readings much below 30°. Give them winter shelter in a deep cold frame that reaches below the frost line, a very cool greenhouse or a minimally heated sun porch. Water them even when they are dormant.

WINTER SHELTERS

The daily demands of bonsai are persistent but that, paradoxically enough, is the major source of the trees' appeal. Said comedian Red Skelton of his yard full of bonsai in California, "I take little trees and shape them the way I want rather than trying to shape people."

Sculptured trees of timeless beauty

A famous 15th Century Japanese play tells of an impoverished samurai who burns his favorite bonsai to warm the hands of a stranger on a cold winter's night. That the Japanese regarded this as a major sacrifice reflects their great love for these diminutive trees and shrubs—a love many Western gardeners now share.

Defined simply, bonsai is the art of dwarfing a tree or shrub by confining it to a small tray or pot and systematically pruning its roots and branches. Almost any woody plant can be dwarfed, but the best specimens are those with small leaves, flowers or fruit—such as a flowering crab apple or narrow-leaved evergreen—for whether six or 36 inches tall, the dwarfed plant must appear perfectly proportioned. It must also appear old. Bits of bark are sometimes stripped from the tree's trunk, roots are exposed, branches may be trained downward with copper wire—all to give the illusion of a tree that time has weighted and weathered.

The many different styles and forms of bonsai range from the straight Upright to the curved Cascade. But whether it is a single tree clinging to a rock *(ishizuki)* or several plants in a miniature forest *(yoseuye),* the bonsai must obey the laws of nature. In the windswept forms, trunk and branches must slant in the same direction to create the effect of a lone tree yielding to ceaseless winds. Trees planted in groves usually show the straight trunks, upward-reaching branches and high foliage of their full-grown counterparts.

Bonsai containers are also bound by certain esthetic guidelines, the first being that they must complement, rather than draw attention from, the plant. Deep pots are used for Cascade-style bonsai, long shallow pots for multitrunk or group plantings, unglazed pots for evergreens, and glazed pots for flowering trees and shrubs.

The bonsai on these pages—trained in the United States by gardeners using native or naturalized plants—reflect years of exacting care. But the rewards were well worth it. "You can get close to your wife, your children, your friends," says one bonsai gardener, "but these trees are always the closest to you because they *are* you."

Found naturally dwarfed in the wild, this 300-year-old California juniper has been trained as a bonsai for 16 years. It stands 33 inches tall.

The defiant sweep of this free-spirited bunjin bonsai was dramatized by stripping most of its bark to create the appearance of great age. The tree is a California juniper.

Only 2 inches less than the usual maximum height of bonsai, this 46-inch Montezuma cypress survived a severe infestation of termites and is healthy and thriving 18 years later.

The ever-popular evergreen

Their symbolic association with longevity and their small needle-like leaves make coniferous evergreens traditional favorites with bonsai enthusiasts. These evergreens also adjust well to container growing. Although their roots must be pruned sparingly over the first year or two for the plants to remain healthy, the supple branches and trunks of many conifers are easily trained into bonsai shapes.

Removing this 28-year-old Atlas cedar from its pot to the ground stimulated growth that thickened its trunk. Now trained in a Curved Upright style, it is 30 inches tall.

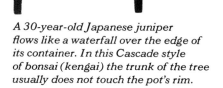

A 30-year-old Japanese juniper flows like a waterfall over the edge of its container. In this Cascade style of bonsai (kengai) the trunk of the tree usually does not touch the pot's rim.

A San Jose juniper 20 years old and 20 inches tall stretches upward in a sinewy V. The trunks of this style of bonsai, called sokan, are said to be "patient and faithful to each other."

A bonsai for all seasons

Deciduous trees and shrubs are popular as bonsai, for their seasonal changes are magical to watch. A crab-apple tree small enough to balance in your hand will send forth flowers in the spring and fruit in the summer, then present a starkly dramatic pattern of bare limbs for your winter pleasure. The delicate features of wild species make them better suited to bonsai rules of proportion than large-fruited varieties.

Bright clusters of May blossoms engulf the gnarled branches of a 30-year-old flowering quince. This 10-inch-tall plant will bear tiny apple-like fruits that will last until frost.

A single Chinese elm 23 inches high spreads its many trunks into a fan shape, reflecting the bonsai belief that each tree should have spaces "for the birds to fly through."

Trained for 20 years in the popular slanted style (shakan), this apple tree is an excellent subject for bonsai because of its naturally crooked trunk and small leaves.

Splashed with the amber color of fall, this Japanese beech tree stands 24 inches tall. Its silvery trunk, wide branches and shallow roots make it a good bonsai selection.

All but a handful of leaves have fallen from this 36-inch elm. Copper wires will be used to train the branches horizontally to create an even more open appearance.

Mystic groves

In *yoseuye* bonsai, the overall effect of the miniature forest or grove is more important than the beauty of any individual tree. Although the group planting should include one tree that is larger than the rest, to serve as a focal point, only in rare instances should that tree dominate the scene. The Japanese usually use an odd number of trees in a forest planting to create a feeling of asymmetry.

Five Chinese elms (two small ones are hidden behind the tree at left) rise from a shallow tray. Chinese elms can reach a height of 50 feet, but the largest one here is only 10 inches tall.

Every two years, these 30-year-old Foemina junipers are wrapped with wire to enhance the twisted look of their trunks. The tallest in the group is only 30 inches in height.

87

This planting of Japanese mountain maples breaks the custom of not letting one tree dominate. The large tree, 30 years old, was trained in the ground for 15 years before being potted.

*Spiky winterberry holly shrubs,
trained for 20 years as bonsai, reveal
stark winter silhouettes. In fall, the
holly bears small red fruits that often
cling until midwinter.*

Rooting trees on rocks

Tiny trees grown on rocks, called *ishizuki* bonsai, suggest miniature islands or craggy mountainsides. A tree can be grown with roots either running over the rock into soil below or anchored in a rock crevice filled with rich soil. Only young trees with vigorous roots are used. The rock, plant and container are chosen carefully to complement one another; rocks blanketed with moss or lichens are especially prized.

The gnarled roots of a 15-year-old azalea cling to a rock. The roots were covered with mud and sphagnum moss, which were removed gradually to force the roots to grow into the soil.

Although this raft-style bonsai appears to consist of several trees, it is a single prostrate juniper. Its trunk was laid horizontally in soil and its branches trained as separate trees.

An azalea (left), a Chinese juniper (top and right) and a Christmas fern (center) are planted in rock crevices to create a tiny island. The rock and a small boat share a basin of water.

This 24-inch jade plant, a bonsai for six years, would normally grow to a height of about 3 feet indoors. Moss and baby's tears at the plant's base echo the bright leaves above.

雪天漫喜歡花梅

Bringing bonsai indoors

Bonsai are usually outdoor plants, brought indoors for only a day or two at a time. But recently the roster of suitable candidates has included tropical and subtropical plants, such as the podocarpus, ficus and gardenia, which require a brief dormant period or none at all and can stay indoors year round. They need humidity and bright indirect light and should be kept away from radiators or hot-air ducts.

A 15-year-old Natal plum, 7 inches tall and bearing green fruit, slopes gently out of a moss-topped pot. Its small foliage and fruit make it a good choice for an indoor bonsai.

Started from seed 15 years ago, three sago palms are now only 18 inches tall. In their native tropics these spiky fronds would wave from heights of 10 feet or more.

Miniatures of miniatures

Bonsai trees small enough to fit in a vest pocket or balance on a fingertip are called *mame* (pronounced mah-may) bonsai. They are difficult to maintain, because their roots, often snuggled in thimble-sized pots, need frequent watering (up to five times daily in summer) and the plants must be repotted annually. *Mame* bonsai are under 7 inches tall and are often displayed with companion plants.

Supporting a fragile canopy of blossoms, a pyracantha 6½ inches tall stands amid a ground cover of moss. The companion plant at left, a dwarf scouring rush, accents the display.

This traditional and elegant arrangement of mame bonsai includes (clockwise from lower left) a five-year-old Hinoki false cypress, an eight-year-old Japanese garden juniper, a waterfall rock, a companion fern and a five-year-old Japanese zelkova.

The towering two-year-old fig tree at right was propagated by planting a cutting from the minuscule 12-year-old mame bonsai displayed with a rock below. Since most bonsai are not genetic miniatures, cuttings taken from them will readily grow to full height. The tree at right will eventually stretch to a height of 4 to 6 feet and bear leaves up to 4 inches long.

An illustrated encyclopedia of miniatures 5

While tiny plants have been known for as long as man has recorded botanical data, collecting and cultivating miniatures for their own sake is a relatively new gardening hobby. The following encyclopedia describes 95 plants that are genetically miniature, dwarfed or naturally very small, lists their uses and discusses their culture. Each illustration includes dimensions to help you visualize how small that plant actually is.

Like collectors of antiques or art, those enchanted with perfection in tiny packages accept the challenge of locating miniatures because they know such plants are unique. All of the plants described in this chapter are commercially available, but few are likely to be available at your nearby nursery. As the demand for them grows, miniatures will find their way into stores carrying a general line of plants. In the meantime, gardeners must search for them.

One good place to start looking for miniature plants is in the classified advertising section of a gardening magazine. Some mail-order nurseries stock only miniatures or small plants for rock gardens. Others may carry miniature varieties of whatever plants they specialize in; an African violet grower, for example, may have some miniature varieties available. Nursery or greenhouse listings in your telephone directory may also turn up speciality growers. Arboretums, botanical gardens and university horticultural departments often have current lists of specialized plant suppliers. Garden clubs in your area may be able to provide the names of members willing to trade miniature plants, share cuttings or reveal their plant sources.

While some small plants can be found growing wild, avoid the temptation to collect your own specimens. A number of alpine plants are endangered species, and many of them cannot be transplanted successfully. (Plants particularly suitable for artificial miniaturization with bonsai techniques, including evergreen and deciduous trees and shrubs, are listed on page 72.)

Shown actual size, these small fruits and plants suggest the wealth of miniature plants available. From upper left, clockwise, they are tomato, ivy, crocus, strawberry, lobularia, African violet and saxifrage.

GREEK ANEMONE
Anemone blanda 'Radar'

Height 3 to 5 in. Flower 2 in.

GLORY-OF-THE-SNOW
Chionodoxa sardensis

Height 3 to 6 in. Flower ¾ in.

Bulbs

ANEMONE

A. blanda (Greek anemone, Grecian windflower); *A. fulgens* (flame anemone, scarlet windflower)

Bright miniature anemones grow from 3 to 10 inches tall, about half the height of the common poppy-flowered anemone. Ideally suited for rock gardens and small patio plantings, they show off flowers 2 inches wide surrounded by deeply cut foliage. They bloom in early spring, long before most other flowers appear. Greek anemones grow 3 to 5 inches tall from tubers that resemble small twigs. The daisy-like flowers often last three weeks. Those of the species are deep blue; the variety Radar has deep rose flowers with white centers; White Splendour produces white flowers that have a silvery sheen when the buds are closed. Flame anemones grow 8 to 10 inches tall from claw-shaped tubers. Their bright red single flowers have dark purple stamens.

Anemones open only in sunlight, closing at night and on cloudy days. As cut flowers they are long-lasting; their stems should be cut close to the ground, not pulled or snapped, to avoid injuring the tubers.

HOW TO GROW. Greek anemones are hardy in Zones 6-9 but can be grown farther north if given a deep winter mulch of salt hay or wood chips. Flame anemones grow best in Zones 9 and 10 on the West Coast where the spring is long and cool and the summer is dry. They grow as far north as Zone 7 if planted in the fall. From Zone 6 northward, they must be planted in the very early spring, then dug up in the late summer and stored at 55° to 60° in dry peat moss, perlite or vermiculite for replanting the following spring.

Both species thrive in partial shade, or in full sun provided they are shielded from the hottest sun in southern areas. A well-drained slightly acid soil, enriched with compost, is ideal for them. Set Greek anemone tubers 4 to 6 inches apart and cover with 2 to 4 inches of soil. Place flame anemone tubers claw-down about 8 inches apart, covering them with 3 to 4 inches of soil. Propagate by dividing the tubers in late summer after the foliage has matured. Plants grown from seeds need about 18 months to reach blooming size. Anemones usually are grown in a greenhouse because they require night temperatures between 35° and 40° to bloom.

ANGEL'S TEARS DAFFODIL See *Narcissus*

BANDED CROCUS See *Crocus*

CHIONODOXA

C. luciliae; C. sardensis (both called chionodoxa, glory-of-the-snow)

Only 3 to 6 inches tall, chionodoxas are alpine bulbs that produce dainty star-shaped flowers and narrow spears of foliage. They bloom in early spring and last two to three weeks if grown in partial shade. In the mountains of Asia Minor, the tiny plants burst into bloom at the edge of melting snow. *C. luciliae*, the more popular species, produces eight to 10 violet-blue flowers on a single stem, each white-centered and up to 1 inch wide. A white variety, *C. luciliae alba*, and a violet-pink, *C. luciliae rosea*, have only two or three flowers per stem. The flowers of *C. sardensis* are only ¾ inch wide; they are bright blue with six to eight on each stem. All chionodoxas are long-lasting as cut flowers.

HOW TO GROW. Chionodoxas are hardy throughout Zones 3-10, but grow best in cool regions. They will multiply and spread in any well-drained soil in full sun or partial shade, provided they have adequate moisture. Set bulbs in the ground in early fall. Place them 1 to 3 inches apart and cover them with at least 3 inches of soil. Since they seldom require fertilizing, they can be left undisturbed after planting. Although chionodoxas can be propagated by division, bulbs are so inexpensive that it is simpler to plant new ones.

CROCUS
C. chrysanthus 'Lady Killer'; *C. chrysanthus* 'Cream Beauty'; *C. sieberi* 'Hubert Edelsten' (Sieber crocus); *C. versicolor; C. zonatus,* also called *C. kotschyanus* (banded crocus) (all called crocus)

Naturally small plants, crocuses grow and spread easily in outdoor rock gardens and flower borders. Although regarded as the herald of spring, there are species that bloom in the fall and some that flower during winter in mild climates. Grown indoors in pots, they can be forced into bloom in midwinter. Goblet-shaped flowers only an inch or two wide open atop 2- to 6-inch stems before the grasslike 8- to 10-inch leaves are fully grown. Crocus flowers come in shades of purple, blue, yellow and white, sometimes striped and usually with prominent yellow or orange anthers.

Of the crocuses listed above, all but the banded crocus bloom in the spring. Lady Killer has dark purple flower cups edged and lined with white. Cream Beauty has an ivory interior and a pale lilac-to-tan exterior. Hubert Edelsten is lilac with an orange throat while *C. versicolor* is striped white and purple with a yellow throat. The fall-blooming banded crocus has rose to lilac petals and a yellow throat.

HOW TO GROW. All crocuses are hardy in Zones 3-10 but grow best from Zone 7 north where winters are cold. They thrive in any well-drained soil in full sun or partial shade. Choose a sunny, sheltered location when early spring flowers are desired; plant in partial shade or on the north side of a building or hedge for later flowering. Spring-blooming crocuses should be planted as early in the fall as possible, fall-blooming kinds in the late summer. Space the corms 2 to 6 inches apart and plant them 2 to 4 inches deep. Dust the soil lightly with bone meal or 5-10-5 fertilizer after planting and repeat this feeding every fall. Allow the foliage to wither before removing it, or the corms may not bloom again the following year. The corms multiply readily by developing small offsets. Some gardeners dig up and divide the corms every three to four years, but they can be left undisturbed. Crocuses also reseed themselves; corms that start from seeds take three to four years to reach flowering size.

To force crocuses into midwinter bloom indoors, plant dormant corms in fall, grouping 10 to 15 of them in a shallow 5- to 7-inch-wide container such as a bulb pan. Use a commercial potting soil or a mixture of 1 part packaged potting soil, 1 part peat moss and 1 part sharp builder's sand, adding a teaspoon of bone meal to each pot. Cover the corms with an inch of soil and keep the soil moist but not soggy. Keep the pots in a cold frame, cellar, or refrigerator at 40° to 50° for 13 weeks or more while roots develop and their need for chilling is satisfied. Then move them indoors to a sunny location where night temperatures are 40° to 50° and day temperatures are about 65°. Plant the corms outside after they flower and they will revert to their natural cycle.

CYCLAMEN-FLOWERED DAFFODIL See *Narcissus*

DAFFODIL See *Narcissus*

DAHLIA
D. hybrids (miniature and pompon dahlias)

For colorful summer flowers in profusion, the small dahlias are popular because they are easier to grow than their larger

Height 2 to 6 in. Flower 1 to 2 in.

SPRING-FLOWERING CROCUS
Crocus versicolor

Height 4 to 6 in. Flower 1 to 2 in.

AUTUMN-FLOWERING CROCUS
Crocus zonatus

Height 2 to 4 ft. Flower 2½ to 4 in.

FORMAL DECORATIVE DAHLIA
Dahlia hybrid 'Bright Spot'

Height 2 to 4 ft. Flower 2½ to 4 in.

STRAIGHT CACTUS DAHLIA
Dahlia hybrid 'Ida Lois'

For climate zones, see map, page 151.

House plants, page 123;   Orchids, page 131;   Rock garden plants, page 134;   Roses, page 143;   Vegetables and fruits, page 145.

Height 2 to 4 ft. Flower 3½ to 4 in.

WATERLILY DAHLIA
Dahlia hybrid 'Nepos'

Height 3 to 5 ft. Flower 1 to 2 in.

POMPON DAHLIA
Dahlia hybrid 'Pom of Poms'

Height 8 in. Flower 1¼ in.

PAGODA FAWN LILY
Erythronium 'Pagoda'

counterparts and they require no staking. Both miniature and pompon dahlias flower from midsummer to frost.

Miniature dahlias bear long-lasting flowers 2½ to 4½ inches wide on plants 2 to 4 feet tall. They come in a wide variety of colors and duplicate the shapes of most of the large dahlias. Four popular categories are the formal decorative dahlias, whose flowers have petals of equal length arranged symmetrically; the waterlily dahlias, which have flat, symmetrically arranged petals with a few upright near the center of the flower, like their namesake; informal decorative dahlias, whose long petals are usually twisted and irregularly spaced; and straight cactus dahlias, whose petals are open at the base but begin to roll into tubelike tips near the center. A sampling of varieties follows: Bright Spot, a yellow formal decorative; Ida Lois, a golden peach straight cactus; Kimberley Robbin, a dark pink formal decorative; Marian K., a yellow, orange or white informal decorative with notched petals; Nepos, a pink waterlily; Rita Robuck, a red formal decorative; and two white varieties, Snow Fairy, a straight cactus, and White Fawn, a formal decorative.

Pompon dahlias have lushly petaled globular flowers only 1 to 2 inches wide. They produce as many as 20 flowers at one time on wiry stems from 3 to 5 feet tall. The following varieties are attractive either massed in gardens or in bouquets: Andrew Lockwood, lavender; Little Willo, white; Pom of Poms, red; Poppet, orange; and Rose Willo, purple.

HOW TO GROW. Small dahlias can be grown almost anywhere in the United States and southern Canada if their roots are protected from frost. In Zone 10 they may be planted in late summer for winter bloom. Elsewhere, dahlias must be planted in the spring, dug in the fall and stored over the winter in a frost-free place.

Dahlias thrive in bright sunlight but will grow in partial shade where they receive at least three hours of sunlight a day. Well-drained soil rich in organic matter, phosphorus and potash suits these plants; where soil is deficient dig in compost or leaf mold and fertilize with 0-20-20 fertilizer.

Growers usually sell dahlias in three forms: pot roots, which are tiny clusters of roots that have come from stem cuttings and matured in small pots; green plants, young dahlias 4 to 6 inches tall that have been started from stem cuttings; and root divisions, tubers separated from parent plants. To plant root divisions, dig holes 7 inches deep, lay the tubers on their sides and cover with 2 inches of soil. As shoots develop, gradually add more soil to fill up each hole. Set green plants or pot roots in the ground in the usual upright position. Space plants 15 to 24 inches apart and water thoroughly. During the growing season keep the plants moist. For bushy plants with several flower stems, pinch off the main stem as soon as four pairs of leaves appear.

After the flowers have faded, dig up the tubers in the fall. Dry them for an hour or so, then place them in a box lined with plastic and filled with dry peat moss, perlite or vermiculite. Store at 40° to 45° to keep the tubers from sprouting.

Propagate from root divisions or stem cuttings. Sow seeds indoors six to eight weeks before the last frost is expected, then set out plants. Seedlings bear flowers the first year.

DANFORD IRIS See *Iris*

ERYTHRONIUM
E. 'Pagoda' (Pagoda fawn lily)

The delicate, lily-like flowers and mottled leaves of the fawn lily show at their best when naturalized in clumps in shady woodland or rock gardens. Pagoda is a Dutch hybrid only 8 inches in height, smaller than either *E. revolutum*

White Beauty or *E. tuolumense,* its foot-tall parents. This miniature bears a cluster of 1¼-inch pale yellow flowers with brown centers atop a single stem in the spring.

HOW TO GROW. The fawn lily grows in Zones 3-9 wherever there are no extremes of heat or dryness. Plant it in partial shade in any moist but well-drained soil. The tiny bulbs should be set out in early fall. Space them 4 to 6 inches apart, cover them with 3 to 4 inches of soil and apply a mulch of coarse peat moss or leaf mold. Renew this mulch every two to three years in the fall. Fawn lilies may be left undisturbed indefinitely or they can be propagated in the fall by digging the bulbs and removing the smaller bulbs that grow around the larger ones. Replant the bulbs immediately so they do not dry out. Started from seed, fawn lilies take two to three years to develop bulbs of flowering size.

FLAME ANEMONE See *Anemone*

FRITILLARIA
F. meleagris (checkered fritillary, guinea-hen flower, snake's-head)

The pattern of purple and white squares on the flowers of the checkered fritillary is a striking sight when these bulbs are massed in floral borders or planted among rough grasses. The solitary, bell-shaped flowers dangle from 6- to 10-inch stems. Before these distinctive 1¼- to 1½-inch flowers open in spring, their broad buds resemble snake's-heads. The variety *alba* is pure white with green veining. Two 6-inch-tall varieties are Contorta, with white-and-purple checked flowers, and Poseidon, white with purple or brown checks.

HOW TO GROW. Checkered fritillary is hardy in Zones 3-10. It grows in full sun or partial shade in a slightly acid soil. Plant the bulbs 3 to 4 inches deep and 3 to 4 inches apart in early fall. When growth begins in the spring, sprinkle a dusting of 5-10-5 fertilizer onto the soil around the plants. Checkered fritillary can be left undisturbed for years, or they can be propagated by digging up the old bulbs in the late spring as soon as the foliage dies, separating the small bulbs growing around them, and replanting the bulbs immediately so that they do not dry out. The tiny bulbs will reach flowering size in a few years.

FRITILLARY See *Fritillaria*

GALANTHUS
G. irkariae, G. nivalis (both called snowdrop)

Dainty white snowdrops make delicate accents when scattered amid rough grasses or planted beneath trees in a woodland setting. They are one of the first flowers to appear in the spring and can be forced into midwinter bloom indoors. Their papery flowers, composed of three green-tipped inner petals and three all-white outer petals, dangle from slender 4- to 8-inch stalks. Their narrow 3- to 8-inch leaf blades die down to the ground by late spring. *G irkariae* bears moss-scented flowers 1¾ inches across. *G. nivalis* has 1-inch flowers; the variety S. Arnott is noteworthy for its sweet fragrance while Flore-Pleno has double-petaled blooms.

HOW TO GROW. Snowdrops are hardy outdoors in Zones 3-9 but grow best in northern zones where winters are cold. During the fall, plant the bulbs 2 to 4 inches apart and 3 to 4 inches deep in partial shade in any well-drained soil. Protect them in the winter by mulching with 2 inches of leaf mold. Snowdrops can be left undisturbed for many years and will multiply rapidly, or older bulbs can be dug up and divided after they have flowered. Replant them immediately so they do not dry out. Snowdrops also spread slowly by self-seeding;

Height 6 to 10 in. Flower 1¼ to 1½ in.

CHECKERED FRITILLARY
Fritillaria meleagris

Height 4 to 8 in. Flower 1 to 2 in.

COMMON SNOWDROP
Galanthus nivalis

For climate zones, see map, page 151.

House plants, page 123;   Orchids, page 131;   Rock garden plants, page 134;   Roses, page 143;   Vegetables and fruits, page 145.

Height to 3 ft. Single floret 2½ in.

MINIATURE GLADIOLUS
Gladiolus hortulanus 'River Styx,' 'Nugget,' 'Amy Beth'

Height 4 to 6 in. Flower 1½ in.

DANFORD IRIS
Iris danfordiae

bulbs that develop from seed take three to four years to reach flowering size.

For midwinter blooms indoors, plant the bulbs in the fall in a mixture of 1 part peat moss, 1 part commercial potting soil and 1 part sharp builder's sand or perlite with a teaspoon of bone meal added to each pot. Set 10 to 15 bulbs ½ inch deep in a 7-inch pot. Water thoroughly, then hold the pot at 40° to 50° in a cold frame, cellar or refrigerator for 13 weeks or more. For flowering, bring the pot into indirect or curtain-filtered sunlight in a location where temperatures are cool, ideally under 50°. Keep the soil moist but not soggy. Planted outdoors after flowering, snowdrops revert to their natural cycle and may bloom the following year.

GLADIOLUS
G. hortulanus (miniature gladiolus)

Providing brightly colored flower spikes for summer bouquets, miniature gladioluses are hardier and easier to grow than their large counterparts. Classified by flower size rather than height, these gladioluses have small florets less than 3½ inches wide; 10 to 20 of these may appear in sequence on one elegant spike. Individual flowers open gradually over a period of a week to 10 days. Planting at intervals of two weeks provides bloom throughout the summer. Flower spikes grow from 2 to 3 feet tall.

Miniature gladioluses come in a variety of colors. The swordlike leaves remain green until frost. The following are recommended for fullness and color: Amy Beth, with ruffled lavender and white florets; Campfire, with deep orange-red florets that have ruffled gold edges; Littlest Angel, creamy white; Nugget, which has florets of deep yellow; Red Bantam, with bright red flowers; and River Styx, with blooms a smooth smoky brown.

HOW TO GROW. These miniatures can be grown year round in Zones 8-10 but will bloom best if the corms are dug and reset each year. They can be grown as far north as Zone 5 if corms are dug and stored indoors for the winter. Gladioluses thrive in full sun and will grow in any garden soil that has been enriched with compost, leaf mold or peat moss; a light sandy loam with a pH of 6.0 to 6.5 is best. Whatever the soil, add 5-10-5 or 5-10-10 fertilizer, adding 1 cup to the soil for each 25-foot row well before planting the corms.

For continuous bloom, plant corms at intervals of seven to 10 days, beginning after the last spring frost and continuing until two months before the first frost is expected. In Zones 9 and 10 where summers are hot (except along the California coast), plant corms from November to February for blooms from January to May. Plant the bulbs 3 inches apart and cover them with 3 to 5 inches of soil. Fertilize them as soon as the spikes appear and again after flowers have been cut. Water thoroughly.

To keep the stems from breaking, pile the soil into 6-inch mounds around the plants once they are 1 foot tall, or support the stems with stakes. At this time apply a 1-inch mulch of straw, salt hay, buckwheat hulls or wood chips around each plant to conserve moisture. Cut the flower spikes in early morning or late afternoon when two or three florets have opened. Leave four to five leaves on each plant.

Four to six weeks after the flowers fade or after the first frost, dig up the corms with a spading fork. Cut off the foliage and place the corms in a shallow container. Let them dry in an airy place out of the sun for two to three weeks. Save any little cormels that have developed. These will grow to flowering size in about two years. Sprinkle the corms and cormels with a combination fungicide-insecticide and store at 40° to 50° over the winter.

GLORY-OF-THE-SNOW See *Chionodoxa*
GRECIAN WINDFLOWER See *Anemone*
GREEK ANEMONE See *Anemone*
GUINEA-HEN FLOWER See *Fritillaria*

HOOPSKIRT DAFFODIL See *Narcissus*

IRIS
I. danfordiae (Danford iris); *I. reticulata* (netted iris)

The flower stalks of these dwarf irises are only 4 to 6 inches tall, yet each bulb produces a flower 1 to 3 inches wide. Blooms appear before leaves have fully developed in the early spring. Danford iris is 4 to 6 inches tall. Its lemon-yellow flowers with olive-green spots appear very early and last a week or two. When flowers fade, the swordlike foliage continues to grow, becoming 12 to 18 inches tall, then dies down in summer. Netted iris grows 4 inches tall with equally tall leaves that develop after the flowers. Its flowers are deep purple and last for one to two weeks. Its varieties come in shades ranging from light to dark purple.

HOW TO GROW. Danford and netted irises are hardy in Zones 5-10. They grow best in full sun but need partial shade when the sun is strongest in Zones 9 and 10. Well-drained, sandy soil is ideal. Plant the bulbs in early fall, spacing them 2 to 3 inches apart and covering them with about 3 inches of soil. When the leaves begin to appear in the spring, dust the soil around them with 5-10-5 fertilizer. Leave the bulbs undisturbed.

Danford irises will spread by themselves, with each bulb splitting into smaller ones. To propagate netted irises, dig up the small bulbs that develop each year and replant them.

JONQUIL See *Narcissus*

LILY, PAGODA FAWN See *Erythronium*

NARCISSUS
N. bulbocodium conspicuus (petticoat daffodil, hoopskirt daffodil); *N. canaliculatus; N. cyclamineus* (cyclamen-flowered daffodil); *N. cyclamineus* 'Tete-a-tete' (Tete-a-tete daffodil); *N. nanus* 'Little Gem'; *N. pumilis plenus* 'Rip Van Winkle'; *N. triandrus albus* (angel's tears daffodil)

Miniature daffodils have a special charm. The little bulbs produce flowers with cups an inch or less in depth, on stalks 3 to 12 inches' tall. They bloom in spring in the garden, and they can be forced into bloom indoors in midwinter. The blooms last two to four weeks.

Petticoat daffodils grow 6 inches tall. Each bulb bears a single flower with a golden-yellow cup that fans out like a tiny hoopskirt, ½ to ¾ inch deep. Their slender leaves are 12 to 15 inches tall and grow during autumn and winter. *N. canaliculatus* grows 6 to 8 inches tall and produces from three to six mildly fragrant flowers 1 inch deep, their white outer petals rimming a tiny deep-yellow cup. The cyclamen-flowered daffodil is 4 to 6 inches tall. Its pale yellow outer petals sweep back about ¼ inch to reveal a ragged-edged, trumpet-like yellow cup, ½ inch deep. The Tete-a-tete variety, 6 to 8 inches tall, bears double yellow flowers.

Little Gem blooms on stalks 3 to 6 inches tall; its twisted outer petals are pale yellow, its cup a deeper hue. The single flowers are ½ to 1 inch deep. Rip Van Winkle grows 7 inches tall and bears small yellow flowers. Angel's tears daffodil produces clusters of three to nine nodding white flowers on stalks 6 to 8 inches tall. Its small outer petals, ½ to ¾ inch long, sweep backward, exposing a ½-inch-deep cup that looks like a tiny teardrop.

For climate zones, see map, page 151.

Height 6 in. Flower ¾ in.

PETTICOAT DAFFODIL
Narcissus bulbocodium conspicuus

Height 6 to 8 in. Flower 1 in.

Narcissus canaliculatus

Height 4 to 6 in. Flower ¾ in.

CYCLAMEN-FLOWERED DAFFODIL
Narcissus cyclamineus

Height 6 to 8 in. Flower ¾ in.

TETE-A-TETE DAFFODIL
Narcissus cyclamineus 'Tete-a-Tete'

House plants, page 123;   Orchids, page 131;   Rock garden plants, page 134;   Roses, page 143;   Vegetables and fruits, page 145.

Height 7 in. Flower 1¼ in.

Height 6 to 8 in. Flower 1¼ in.

Narcissus pumilis plenus
'Rip Van Winkle'

ANGEL'S TEARS DAFFODIL
Narcissus triandus albus

Height 6 to 12 in. Flower 1 in.

COMMON STAR-OF-BETHLEHEM
Ornithogalum umbellatum

HOW TO GROW. Miniature daffodils are hardy outdoors in Zones 6-10. All kinds grow best in full sun but also grow well in partial shade; petticoat, cyclamen-flowered and angel's tears daffodils are among the best for a shady location. All thrive in well-drained soil except cyclamen-flowered daffodil, which prefers damp soil. In late summer, plant bulbs in holes 6 inches deep, spaced about 3 inches apart. Work a level teaspoonful of bone meal into the soil of each hole. When shoots appear in the spring, lightly scatter 5-10-5 fertilizer around the plants. Be careful not to mistake grasslike leaves for weeds and pull them out. Propagate by separating and replanting small bulbs that form around the larger ones.

For midwinter bloom indoors, plant bulbs in the fall in a bulb pan or shallow container filled with commercial potting soil to within an inch of the top. Place the bulbs in a cold frame, a refrigerator or a cellar at 40° to 48° for 15 weeks. Then move the plants indoors to a sunny window. Once buds appear, move them into indirect or curtain-filtered sunlight. They will grow best, and their blooms will remain longest, at temperatures of 50° to 55° at night and 68° or lower in the daytime. Keep flowering plants moist but not soggy.

NETTED IRIS See *Iris*

ORNITHOGALUM
O. umbellatum (star-of-Bethlehem)

Often planted among grasses, star-of-Bethlehem is a rugged, bulbous perennial. Its fragrant flowers, star shaped and white, are an inch wide and appear in flat clusters of 12 to 20 in late spring; indoors they can be brought into bloom in midwinter. The slender leaves, ⅓ inch wide, grow 6 to 12 inches tall; they quickly die to the ground after flowering. Star-of-Bethlehem often spreads and pushes out other plants.

HOW TO GROW. Hardy in Zones 4-10, star-of-Bethlehem grows in full sun or partial shade and tolerates any well-drained soil. Plant bulbs in the fall; space them 3 to 4 inches apart and cover them with 3 to 4 inches of soil.

For midwinter blooming indoors, plant bulbs in the fall. Pot them 1 inch deep in a mixture of equal parts commercial potting soil, coarse sand and peat moss. Provide 13 to 14 weeks of temperatures 40° to 48°, in a refrigerator or cold frame. Then place the bulbs where they will receive at least four hours of direct sunlight a day, with temperatures of 50° to 60° at night and 68° to 72° during the day. Keep the soil evenly moist but not soggy until bloom starts, then let it become slightly dry between thorough waterings. While the foliage is green, feed monthly with a standard house-plant fertilizer. After flowering, move the bulbs to the garden and let them rest by withholding both water and fertilizer.

PETTICOAT DAFFODIL See *Narcissus*

SCARLET WINDFLOWER See *Anemone*
SIEBER CROCUS See *Crocus*
SNAKE'S-HEAD See *Fritillaria*
SNOWDROP See *Galanthus*
STAR-OF-BETHLEHEM See *Ornithogalum*

TULIP See *Tulipa*

TULIPA
T. fosteriana 'Princeps'; *T. greigi* 'Cape Cod,' 'Plaisir' and 'Red Riding Hood'; *T. kaufmanniana* 'Mendelssohn,' 'Orange Boy' and 'Joseph Kafka'; *T. kolpakowskiana; T. pulchella violacea; T. tarda,* also called *T. dasystemon; T. turkestanica* (all called miniature tulip)

These low-growing tulips come in a wide range of colors, blooming outdoors from March through May, depending on the locality, and in the house during midwinter. They range from 3 to 8 inches tall, producing flowers 1 to 4 inches wide. Princeps is an early-blooming tulip that grows 8 inches tall; its red flowers, 3 to 4 inches wide, are daubed inside with yellow. The *T. greigi* hybrids are late-blooming tulips with green leaves mottled with purple or brown. Cape Cod has yellow flowers bronzed inside and flushed with orange-red on the outside, and Red Riding Hood has solid red flowers; both plants grow up to 8 inches tall. Plaisir is 6 inches tall; its red flowers are edged with pale yellow.

T. kaufmanniana tulips flower early. They range from 4 to 8 inches tall; their broad leaves are usually striped with brown. Often called waterlily tulips, they have pointed petals that form blooms 3½ inches wide. The yellow-and-rose variety Mendelssohn grows 5 inches tall, as does Orange Boy, solid orange, and Joseph Kafka, which bears yellow flowers flushed with red. *T. kolpakowskiana* grows 6 inches tall; its yellow flowers are 2¼ inches wide and are shaded on their outer surfaces with red or olive.

T. pulchella flower stalks grow only 4 inches tall amid slender 6-inch leaves. The small star-shaped blooms are 1¼ inches wide. The variety Violet is cup-shaped. *T. tarda*, an early-flowering species, grows about 3 inches tall; a single stalk may produce three to five flowers, each 1½ inches wide, with pointed petals. *T. turkestanica*, another early-flowering tulip, grows 6 to 8 inches tall; its flowers are white within the cup and yellow and green on the outside. Five to nine blooms, each 2 inches wide, are carried on one stem.

HOW TO GROW. Miniature tulips are hardy in Zones 3-7 and also are grown in the West and Southwest in Zones 8-10. All thrive in full sun but grow well if they receive at least five hours of direct sunlight a day. They will grow in any well-drained soil supplemented with ½ teaspoonful of bone meal worked into the soil of each hole in which a bulb is set. Plant bulbs in the early fall, spacing them 3 to 6 inches apart and covering them with 3 to 6 inches of soil. In the spring when leaves appear, scatter 5-10-5 fertilizer lightly on the soil around the plants.

To start small tulips indoors, plant them in early fall. Set them in commercial potting soil. Fill a bulb pan or pot to within 2 inches of the top, and press the bulbs into the soil until they are well covered, setting them ½ inch apart. Water thoroughly after planting. Place planted bulbs in a cold frame, refrigerator or cellar at 40° to 48°. Leave early-flowering bulbs for at least 13 weeks and late-flowering bulbs for 16 weeks. Then move the plants to a sunny window. Once buds appear, move the tulips to indirect sunlight so flowers will last longer. Maintain night temperatures of 50° to 65° and day temperatures at 68° or lower. The cooler the air, the longer flowers will last.

Cacti and succulents

ALOE

A. descoingsii (miniature aloe)

A slow-growing succulent for a desert dish garden, this miniature aloe forms stemless rosettes of white-spotted fleshy leaves edged with prickly white spines. The leaves arch outward and fold inward. A single rosette may measure 1 to 2 inches across. This miniature aloe sends up 5- to 6-inch stalks with scarlet to vermilion flowers about ¼ to ½ inch long that last for about a week.

HOW TO GROW. This aloe grows best with four or more hours of direct sunlight a day, or 12 to 14 hours of strong

Height 6 in. Flower 2¼ in.

MINIATURE TULIP
Tulipa kolpakowskiana

Height 4 in. Flower 1¼ in.

MINIATURE TULIP
Tulipa pulchella

Height 4 in. Flower 1¼ in.

MINIATURE TULIP
Tulipa pulchella 'Violacea'

Height 3 to 4 in. Flower 1½ in.

MINIATURE TULIP
Tulipa tarda

For climate zones, see map, page 151.

House plants, page 123;   Orchids, page 131;   Rock garden plants, page 134;   Roses, page 143;   Vegetables and fruits, page 145.

Rosette diameter 1 to 2 in. Flower length ¼ to ½ in.

MINIATURE ALOE
Aloe descoingsii

Rosette diameter 1½ in. Flower stalk length 6 in.

MINIATURE HEN-AND-CHICKENS
Echeveria minima

artificial light; it can also be grown in bright indirect light. Keep humidity low. From spring to fall, when plants are actively growing, temperatures should range from 50° to 55° at night and 68° to 72° by day. In the winter rest period, keep temperatures between 45° and 50° at night and between 60° and 65° by day.

Use a planting mixture of equal parts of commercial potting soil and sharp sand, adding 1 teaspoon of ground limestone and 1 teaspoon of bone meal to each quart of mix. During active growth allow the soil to become dry to the touch between thorough waterings. Increase moisture slightly during flowering. Through the winter rest, water just enough to keep the plant from shriveling. When new growth starts, feed established plants, dusting 1 teaspoon of bone meal around each plant.

Outdoors, this aloe is hardy in Zone 10 and in frost-free areas of Zone 9. Plant in full sun, in sandy well-drained loam. Work ground limestone and bone meal into the soil before planting, and feed with bone meal each year when new growth begins. Propagate at any season from offshoots or sow seeds in late winter or early spring.

BRUCH'S CHIN CACTUS See *Gymnocalycium*

COCKLEBUR See *Huernia*
COLUMNAR PEPEROMIA See *Peperomia*

ECHEVERIA
E. minima (miniature hen-and-chickens)

The miniature hen-and-chickens succulent forms tight, flat rosettes each up to 1½ inches in diameter. They are composed of plump blue leaves with pointed tips that range from red to purple, depending on the intensity of light. Bell-shaped yellow and pink flowers are borne on slender 6-inch stalks. Offshoots readily form at the base of each rosette. *E. minima* is often planted in dish gardens that depict desert landscapes.

HOW TO GROW. This small echeveria grows best with four to six hours of direct sunlight a day or 14 to 16 hours of very bright artificial light. Maintain temperatures of 65° to 70° at night and 70° to 85° in the daytime through spring and summer. In fall and winter lower them to 50° to 65° at night and 65° to 75° by day.

Plant in a mixture of 1 part coarse sand and 1 part packaged potting soil, adding 1 teaspoon of ground limestone and 1 teaspoon of bone meal for each quart of mix. Throughout the growing season allow the soil to become almost dry before watering it thoroughly. In winter, water it just enough to prevent the succulent leaves from shriveling. Be careful not to get water on the leaves, since it will spot them. Withhold fertilizer from new plants or repotted plants for one year; feed established plants once in the spring with a foliage house-plant fertilizer such as 10-20-10 diluted to half the strength recommended on the label.

Outdoors *E. minima* is hardy in Zone 10 and in areas of Zone 9 where it is protected from frost. Propagate miniature hen-and-chickens in spring from offsets.

ECHEVERIA See also *Graptopetalum*

FRAILEA
F. grahliana

Only 1½ inches in diameter, the globe-shaped *F. grahliana* is a tiny cactus well suited for use in a miniature desert landscape, as are most other fraileas. Each plant has 13 ribs from which radiate yellowish spines. Though reluctant to bloom in cultivation, *F. grahliana* may produce yellow flowers 1½ inches long on top of the globe in summer. They are followed by green fruits about ¼ inch in diameter.

HOW TO GROW. Outdoors or indoors, *F. grahliana* grows best if planted in groups in a shallow pan rather than in individual small pots. It prefers a soil that is half leaf mold and half sharp sand. Add 1 teaspoon of ground limestone per quart of mixture. Unlike most cacti, frailea requires indirect light indoors or partial shade outdoors. Let the soil become slightly dry to the touch before you water except during winter dormancy, when you should water only enough to prevent shriveling. Winter temperatures should range from 40° to 50° at night and up to 65° during the day. From spring through autumn, night temperatures should range from 65° to 70° and day temperatures from 75° to 80°. Withhold fertilizer for one year after transplanting; established plants should be fed each spring with a balanced house-plant fertilizer such as 10-10-10, diluted as recommended on the label.

GRAPTOPETALUM
G. macdougallii, also called *Echeveria macdougallii*

Although it is sturdy and easily grown, the *Graptopetalum macdougallii* has a shimmering blue-white coloring that gives it a delicate beauty. A protective waxy powder that covers the succulent leaves provides this coloration. Each ground-hugging rosette bears up to 50 leaves. Each leaf is rounded, with a pointed tip, and is up to 1¾ inches long, ½ inch wide and slightly more than ¼ inch thick. In late winter or early spring the plant sends up a branching 6-inch flower stem. Each of the branches bears several red-striped flowers, each only 1¼ inches wide.

HOW TO GROW. This succulent grows best with four to six hours of direct sunlight daily or very bright artificial light for 14 to 16 hours a day. It also grows fairly well in filtered sunlight or bright reflected light.

Indoors, provide night temperatures of 50° to 65° and day temperatures of 68° to 90° in spring and summer. In fall and winter, temperatures of 40° to 50° at night and 65° or less by day are needed. From spring through autumn, let the soil become almost dry between thorough waterings; in winter, water plants even less, just enough to prevent shriveling.

Do not fertilize newly potted plants for one year; give established plants one spring feeding with a solution of a foliage-house-plant fertilizer such as 10-20-10 diluted to half the strength recommended on the label. Divide and repot crowded plants in any season. Use a mixture of 1 part sharp sand and 1 part commercial potting soil, adding 1 teaspoon each of ground limestone and bone meal for every quart of potting mix. Plants are best propagated in spring from leaf or stem cuttings, seeds or divisions.

Graptopetalum can be summered outdoors and can be grown outdoors year round in Zone 10. Set in light, sandy loam, where it will get abundant sunlight with very little shade in summer. Feed once in the spring with a high-phosphorus fertilizer, following the label directions.

GYMNOCALYCIUM
G. bruchii (Bruch's chin cactus)

The raised, chinlike protuberances below each cluster of spines distinguish this cactus. Up to 2 inches in diameter, this small, spherical cactus forms a cluster of stems as it matures. They are deeply ribbed, with needle-shaped white or brown spines ¼ inch long. Bruch's chin cactus blooms during the spring. The pink to rose-violet, funnel-shaped flowers are up to 2 inches long and 1¼ inches wide. The long-lasting flowers are produced when plants are fairly young—sometimes

Diameter 1½ in. Flower length 1½ in.

Frailea grahliana

Leaf size 1¾ by ½ by ¼ in. Flower width 1¼ in.

Graptopetalum macdougallii

For climate zones, see map, page 151.

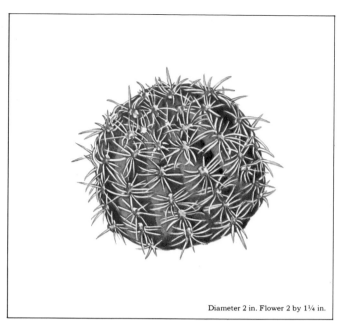

Diameter 2 in. Flower 2 by 1¼ in.

BRUCH'S CHIN CACTUS
Gymnocalycium bruchii

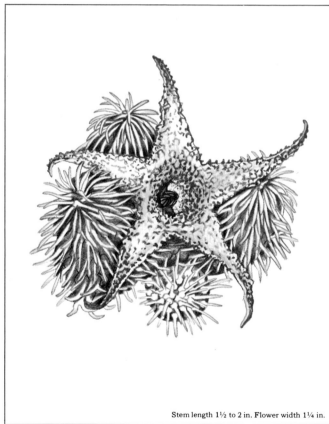

Stem length 1½ to 2 in. Flower width 1¼ in.

COCKLEBUR
Huernia pillansii

on plants less than an inch in diameter and only two or three years old. Bruch's chin cactus is a good choice for beginners as it is easy to grow and to bring into bloom.

HOW TO GROW. Bruch's chin cactus grows best with at least four hours of direct sunlight each day, or in bright artificial light for 14 to 16 hours daily. Night temperatures of 50° to 55° and day temperatures of 68° to 72° year round are ideal. From spring through autumn, water only when the top of the soil in the container feels dry to the touch; in winter, water just enough to keep the plant from shriveling. Fertilize each year in the spring, using a high-phosphorus fertilizer such as 15-30-15, following label instructions. Do not feed newly potted plants for one year. Grow in a potting mix of equal parts of sharp sand and commercial potting soil, adding 1 teaspoon each of ground limestone and bone meal to each quart of mix. Repot in any season when plants are overcrowded; otherwise, repot in spring. Propagate by dividing the clustered stems or from seed at any time of the year.

Bruch's chin cactus can be summered outdoors on a terrace or grown outdoors year round in Zone 10 if protected from frost. Plant in light, sandy soil with full sun most of the year but partial shade in summer. Fertilize annually in the spring, using a high-phosphorus fertilizer such as 15-30-15 and following label instructions.

HEN-AND-CHICKENS See *Echeveria*

HUERNIA

H. pillansii (cocklebur)

The leafless stems of the cocklebur, a succulent, are so covered with bristly teeth that the plant resembles a cactus. A slow-growing plant, it forms tight clusters of finger-like stems 1½ to 2 inches tall. Flowers emerge from the base of each stem in the spring and summer. Shaped like starfish, the 1-inch pale yellow flowers are freckled with red and covered with stiff hairs.

HOW TO GROW. The cocklebur grows best with at least four hours of filtered sunlight each day or eight to 12 hours of strong artificial light. From spring through autumn, temperatures of 65° to 70° at night and from 75° to 85° by day are ideal; in winter, a range from 40° at night to 65° or less during the day is recommended. Cockleburs are susceptible to rot if overwatered. From spring through fall, allow the soil to dry thoroughly between waterings. In winter, water the plants only enough to keep them from shriveling.

Fertilize established plants monthly during the growing season with a balanced house-plant fertilizer such as 10-10-10 diluted to half the strength recommended on the label. Repot in spring if plants become overcrowded in a potting mix composed of equal parts of commercial potting soil and sharp sand with 1 teaspoon of ground limestone and 1 teaspoon of bone meal added to each quart of mix. Do not fertilize newly potted plants during their first year. Propagate by dividing the clumps when the plants are actively growing. Root the divisions in moist vermiculite.

Cockleburs grown as house plants may be placed outdoors in partial shade during the summer. This succulent will grow outdoors year round in frost-free areas of Zone 10 in very well-drained sandy loam and partial shade.

LITTLE CANDLES See *Mammillaria*

MAMMILLARIA

M. prolifera (silver-cluster cactus, little candles)

One of the smallest members of this large and diverse genus of low-growing cacti, the silver-cluster cactus forms a mass of dark green stems as it matures; each stem is 1 to 2 inches thick, about 2½ inches tall, and covered with thin, closely spaced, yellow to brown spines. During spring and summer, small yellow flowers ring the top of the plant, blooming on the previous season's growth. As each flower fades, a cylindrical red fruit develops. The silver-cluster cactus can be grown individually in a pot or in a dish garden.

HOW TO GROW. The silver-cluster cactus grows best indoors where it receives at least four hours of direct sunlight daily or 12 hours of strong artificial light. In winter, night temperatures of 40° to 50° and day temperatures under 65° are ideal; from spring through autumn, temperatures of 60° to 70° at night and 75° to 85° by day are recommended. Let the soil become dry to the touch between waterings from spring through autumn. In the winter, water only enough to keep plants from shriveling; water slightly more often if the cactus is kept in a warm room. Fertilize established plants once a year in the spring, using a high-phosphorus fertilizer such as 15-30-15 at the strength recommended on the label. Repot in early spring if stems become overcrowded, using a mixture of equal parts commercial potting soil and sharp sand with 1 teaspoon of ground limestone and 1 teaspoon of bone meal added to each quart of mix. Do not fertilize newly potted plants the first year. Propagate silver-cluster cacti from offsets or from seed in the spring.

Silver-cluster cactus that is grown as a house plant can be placed outdoors in the summer. It can be grown outdoors year round in Zone 10 in a location with full sun and loose, sandy loam. Feed cacti grown outdoors every year in the spring with a high-phosphorus fertilizer, following the recommendations on the label.

PEPEROMIA

P. columella (columnar peperomia)

The thick, fleshy, bright green leaves of the columnar peperomia are closely packed on 2- to 4-inch upright stems. These stems branch and send up new growth from the base. Occasionally, plants produce diminutive tail-like flowers in spring. Columnar peperomia can be grown in individual pots or it can be combined with other slow-growing miniatures in an indoor dish garden.

HOW TO GROW. Columnar peperomia does best in bright indirect or curtain-filtered sunlight, or in at least 12 hours daily of low to average artificial light. Night temperatures of 65° to 70° and day temperatures of 75° to 85° are recommended. Let the soil become dry to the touch between thorough waterings from spring through fall; in winter, allow the soil to become slightly drier before watering. Feed established plants every other month in spring and summer with a standard house-plant fertilizer such as 10-20-10, diluted to half the strength recommended on the label. Do not feed plants in winter or for four to six months after purchasing or repotting. Although columnar peperomia seldom becomes overcrowded, if necessary repot in early spring when new growth starts. Grow in a mixture of equal parts commercial potting soil and sharp sand with 1 teaspoon of bone meal and 1 teaspoon of ground limestone added to each quart of mix. Propagate from stem cuttings taken in spring or summer.

Columnar peperomia may be summered outdoors in partial shade. Hardy in frost-free areas of Zone 10, its small size limits its use to specialized miniature gardens.

REBUTIA

R. albiflora (white crown cactus)

A free-blooming, easy-to-grow cactus only ½ to ¾ inch in diameter, the gray-green white crown cactus readily sends

Stem size 2½ by 2 in.

SILVER-CLUSTER CACTUS
Mammillaria prolifera

Stem length 2 to 4 in.

COLUMNAR PEPEROMIA
Peperomia columella

For climate zones, see map, page 151.

out offsets, so its container is soon filled with tiny progeny. Fine white spines cover the ribless globe. During spring and summer, inch-wide white flowers emerge from around the base of each globe. A flower lasts two days, opening in the morning and closing at night. Plants bloom when young, usually in two years if grown from seed. Often plants produce so many flowers that they expend themselves and die, but they leave numerous healthy offsets behind.

HOW TO GROW. White crown cactus grows best with four hours or more of direct sunlight each day; during the summer, it should be shaded from hot midday sun. Plants also grow well under strong artificial light, 12 to 16 hours daily. In winter, provide night temperatures of 40° to 45° and day temperatures under 65°. From spring through fall, night temperatures of 50° to 65° and day temperatures of 65° to 85° are recommended. When the plant is actively growing or flower buds are developing, water thoroughly when the soil becomes dry to the touch. During dormancy, water only enough to keep it from shriveling.

Fertilize established plants once each year in the spring with a teaspoon of bone meal or with a standard house-plant fertilizer at half the strength recommended on the label. Do not fertilize newly potted plants for a year. Divide and repot crowded plants in early spring in a mixture of equal parts of commercial potting mix and sharp sand. Add 1 teaspoon of ground limestone and 1 teaspoon of bone meal to each quart of mix. Propagate from seed or from offsets when plants are actively growing.

White crown cactus may be summered outdoors in partial shade. Although hardy in Zone 10, its size limits its outdoor use to miniature gardens and specialized rock gardens.

SILVER-CLUSTER CACTUS See *Mammillaria*

WHITE CROWN CACTUS See *Rebutia*

Evergreens
ALBERTA SPRUCE See *Picea*
AMERICAN ARBORVITAE See *Thuja*
AZALEA See *Rhododendron*

BOX See *Buxus*
BOXWOOD See *Buxus*

BUXUS
B. microphylla (littleleaf boxwood or box); *B. microphylla* 'Compacta' (kingsville dwarf boxwood or box)

Densely foliaged boxwood, which responds well to pruning and shearing, is easy to train as a low hedge, perhaps a foot tall, or as a miniature tree. This compact shrub can also be grown in a container, and the shallow roots of the Kingsville dwarf make it a good choice for bonsai culture. Boxwood has shiny, dark green oval or tongue-shaped leaves that may turn brown in cold weather. The leaves of littleleaf boxwood are about 1 inch long, while those of the Kingsville dwarf are half that size. Littleleaf boxwood may reach a height of 3 feet. The smaller Kingsville dwarf may grow no taller than 1 foot in 40 years, with a spread of up to 4 feet.

HOW TO GROW. Boxwood grows best in areas that do not have extremes of summer heat or winter cold, Zones 5-9 in the eastern half of the United States and Zones 8 and 9 along the Pacific Coast. Give plants moist, well-drained soil and full sun or partial shade. Transplant boxwood outdoors in spring or early autumn, and water well for the first few weeks. A 1-inch mulch of peat, wood chips, peanut shells or

Diameter ½ to ¾ in. Flower width 1 in.

WHITE CROWN CACTUS
Rebutia albiflora

other organic material will prevent damage to the shallow roots that might be caused by weeding. If leaves become pale, scatter cottonseed meal or lawn fertilizer under the plant in early spring.

Indoors, the plants need at least four hours a day of direct sun, but will grow reasonably well in bright indirect light. Winter temperatures of 40° to 55° at night and no more than 65° during the day are best. An unheated, enclosed sun porch would be a good location. Boxwood may be grown in commercial potting soil; keep the soil barely moist at all times. Do not fertilize newly potted plants the first year, but feed established plants annually in early spring, using a balanced foliage-house-plant fertilizer such as 20-20-20.

Boxwood roots readily from both hardwood and softwood cuttings in summer or early autumn. In the colder areas of Zone 5, rooted cuttings should be wintered in a cold frame until transplanted outdoors in late spring.

CANADIAN HEMLOCK See *Tsuga*
CAPE JASMINE See *Gardenia*

CHAMAECYPARIS

C. lawsoniana 'Dow's Gem' (dwarf false cypress); *C. lawsoniana* 'Filiformis Compacta' (compact false cypress); *C. obtusa* 'Caespitosa' (dwarf false cypress); *C. obtusa* 'Nana Gracilis' (dwarf false cypress); *C. pisifera* 'Plumosa Compacta' (compact false cypress); *C. pisifera* 'Squarrosa Intermedia' (intermediate false cypress); *C. thyoides* 'Andelyensis' (spiny white cedar); *C. thyoides* 'Ericoides' (dwarf white cedar)

Dwarf false cypresses and white cedars are among the best trees and shrubs for miniature garden landscapes because they are easy conifers to grow and they offer a wide variety of sizes and shapes from which to choose. Their leaves are usually wedge shaped and small, with the look of tiny overlapping shells; in some varieties the foliage of the young plants is spinelike.

The Dow's Gem variety of Lawson's false cypress is a low, spreading shrub that attains a breadth sometimes greater than its mature height. With drooping branches and feathery gray-blue leaf sprays, this dwarf contrasts markedly with the standard Lawson's false cypress that grows to a height of 150 feet. Filiformis Compacta false cypress forms a dense globe; in 15 years it may be 1½ feet tall and 2½ feet wide. Looking like a wet mop, with cordlike, drooping branches, it has small leaves that are bluish green with white markings. Lawson's false cypress varieties grow best in humid Pacific Coast areas of Zone 5, but they will also grow elsewhere in Zones 6 and 7.

Caespitosa, a petite, bun-shaped dwarf variety of hinoki false cypress, grows slowly to become 5 inches tall and 6 inches broad. It has spreading, shell-shaped branchlets that are densely covered with dark green scalelike leaves. Another dwarf hinoki false cypress, Nana Gracilis, is a compact, conical plant, bushy when young but wider and less shapely at maturity. At 30 years, it may be 4 to 5 feet tall. Lustrous dark green foliage covers the curving, often twisted branchlets. Hinoki false cypresses grow as far north as Zone 5 and will grow in humid areas of Zones 6-8.

Plumosa Compacta, a compact sawara false cypress, grows slowly to a height of 6½ feet, with short, spreading branches covered with foliage that is blue on its upper surface and green underneath. Squarrosa Intermedia, an intermediate moss sawara, forms a loose ball with dense blue foliage. After 20 years, the plant becomes somewhat conical in shape, growing 6½ feet tall. Sawara false cypresses grow in Zones 5 and 6 and in all but dry parts of Zone 7.

For climate zones, see map, page 151.

Size 1 by 4 ft. in 40 years

KINGSVILLE DWARF BOXWOOD
Buxus microphylla 'Compacta'

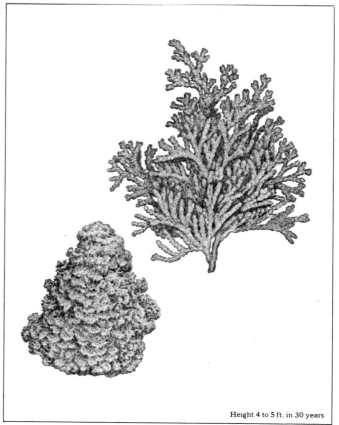

Height 4 to 5 ft. in 30 years

DWARF FALSE CYPRESS
Chamaecyparis obtusa 'Nana Gracilis'

House plants, page 123;   Orchids, page 131;   Rock garden plants, page 134;   Roses, page 143;   Vegetables and fruits, page 145.

The spiny white cedar grows up to 10 feet tall and is conical in shape, with closely spaced branches; its foliage changes from the spiny needles of the young plant to small scalelike leaves as the tree matures. The latter foliage is blue-green in summer and violet red in winter. The tree bears many cones and grows very slowly. Ericoides, a dwarf white cedar, grows only 1 inch per year to a height of about 5 feet. Its blunt-topped conical shape is covered in summer with spiny gray-green leaves that turn plum colored in winter. White cedars grow well in moist areas of Zones 3-9.

HOW TO GROW. The dwarf forms of false cypress and white cedar grow best with full sun in cool, moist climates. All need soil that is moist but well drained and protection from strong wind. Most grow best in slightly acid soil, but some varieties of Lawson's false cypress also grow well in alkaline soil.

Water newly planted trees or shrubs once a week until roots are well established—a period that may extend over two years for slow-growing evergreens. To conserve moisture over the winter, provide an organic mulch about 2 inches deep. This precaution is especially important for container-grown plants in soil that dries faster than garden soil.

Pruning is seldom necessary unless a particular size is desired. For this, thin out the longest branches in late fall or early winter. Since these dwarfs are mutants, one may occasionally put out a branch too large for such a small tree. Such branches should be removed completely.

CHINOTTO See *Citrus*

CITRUS
C. aurantium myrtifolia (myrtle-leaf orange, chinotto)

Ornamental the year around, the myrtle-leaf orange is a dwarf broad-leaved evergreen that branches low and densely from a single trunk and grows about 8 feet tall in 25 years. Its dark green, glossy leaves are about 1½ inches long; very fragrant white flowers ½ inch wide bloom in late winter or early spring. Tiny orange fruits only 1 inch in diameter hang on the tree for months, often while the tree again flowers. Leaves, flowers and fruit grow directly from the thornless branches, not on fruiting spurs.

HOW TO GROW. The myrtle-leaf orange may be grown outdoors in Zones 9 and 10, either in tubs or set in the ground. If used to border a yard or line a walk, trees should be planted 6½ to 8 feet apart. For a dense hedge, space plants 3 to 4 feet apart. Plant them in early spring, summer or early fall in moist soil that is well drained. A mulch of wood chips or ground bark will help keep roots moist. Plant a tub-grown myrtle-leaf orange in a mixture of commercial potting soil and peat moss or leaf mold. Place a layer of coarse gravel in the bottom of the tub to ensure good drainage. If a potted plant is moved indoors, keep temperatures between 50° and 55° at night and 68° and 72° during the day. The tree needs four hours of direct sunlight a day. Pinch back terminal growth to maintain compactness.

COLORADO BLUE SPRUCE See *Picea*
COMMON JUNIPER See *Juniperus*
CREEPING JUNIPER See *Juniperus*

CRYPTOMERIA
C. japonica 'Elegans Nana' (dwarf Japanese cedar); *C. japonica* 'Globosa Nana' (dwarf Japanese cedar); *C. japonica* 'Jindai-Sugi' (dwarf Japanese cedar); *C. japonica* 'Knaptonensis' (dwarf Japanese cedar); *C. japonica* 'Vilmoriana' (dwarf Japanese cedar)

While the shredded red-brown bark and distinctive root

Height 8 ft. in 25 years. Fruit diameter 1 in.

MYRTLE-LEAF ORANGE
Citrus aurantium myrtifolia

Height 3 ft. in 40 years, 6 ft. in 80 years

DWARF JAPANESE CEDAR
Cryptomeria japonica 'Globosa Nana'

formations of the standard Japanese cedar appeal to cultivators of bonsai, its dwarf varieties are popular choices for miniature gardens. Most of these varieties, though diverse in growth habits, have narrow incurved green needles that in winter may turn to colors ranging from bronze to blue.

Elegans Nana, a flattened compact globe with gracefully curving branches, grows slowly to 3½ feet. Its soft blue-green foliage changes to rich purple in winter. Globosa Nana maintains a height of up to 3 feet for as long as 40 years, but may become 6 feet tall at 80. Conical when young, it becomes globelike with age. Its spreading branches are covered with short needles, yellow-green in summer and slightly blue in winter. It withstands winter cold better than other dwarf varieties of Japanese cedar. Jindai-Sugi is a dwarf that grows compactly to about 3½ feet high and 2½ feet wide in 20 years. The upward spreading branches are covered with fine, short, bright green needles that may become slightly bronze in the winter.

Knaptonensis is sometimes conical and sometimes cushion shaped. It grows up to 4 feet tall in 30 years. Young foliage is white, but it usually turns pale green in the second year. Sometimes the young needles twist around the branchlets, but they straighten with age. When carefully tended and protected from wind and extreme cold, Knaptonensis is a singular specimen. Vilmoriana is a low, slowly developing mound suitable for small rock gardens; it grows up to 2½ feet tall in about 40 years. It has short, densely growing light green needles that turn a deep reddish bronze in winter.

HOW TO GROW. Dwarf Japanese cedars grow best in unpolluted air with deep acid soil that is moist and well drained. They are hardy in Zones 8-10 and in warmer coastal areas of Zone 7, though in the latter zone the foliage may turn brownish in winter. Plant dwarf Japanese cedars in the sun but sheltered from the wind. They need protection from low temperatures and from hot, dry summers. Water new plants regularly during their first summer and whenever dry conditions prevail. The roots of young plants should never be allowed to become dry.

DOUGLAS FIR See *Pseudostuga*

EASTERN WHITE PINE See *Pinus*

FALSE CYPRESS See *Chamaecyparis*

GARDENIA
G. jasminoides veitchii (dwarf gardenia, dwarf Cape jasmine)

A house-plant-sized gardenia for a miniature garden outdoors or for a large sunny window, this evergreen shrub grows from 1 to 3 feet tall. It bears fragrant waxy white flowers, 3 inches wide, amid shiny dark green leaves 4 to 6 inches long. Indoors the dwarf gardenia blooms intermittently all year; outdoors it flowers in spring and summer when days are mild and night temperatures do not fall below 65°. A few flowers may appear in fall.

HOW TO GROW. Indoors, dwarf gardenias grow best with four to six hours a day of direct sunlight or 14 to 16 hours a day of strong artificial light. They need temperatures of 60° to 65° at night and 68° to 72° by day, plus humidity between 50 and 60 per cent. To help maintain humidity at this level, place the potted plant on a pebble-filled tray. Keep the pebbles moist but make sure the water level remains below the bottom of the pot. Plant them in a mixture of 2 parts sphagnum peat moss, 1 part vermiculite and 1 part coarse sand or perlite. Keep the mixture moist but never soggy, and fertilize monthly with a balanced house-plant fertilizer such

Height 1 to 3 ft. Flower width 3 in.

DWARF GARDENIA
Gardenia jasminoides veitchii

For climate zones, see map, page 151.

as 20-20-20 at the strength recommended on the label. Propagate from stem cuttings of new growth.

Outdoors, dwarf gardenias grow well in Zones 8-10 in the eastern United States, in Southern California and inland in northern California. They thrive in full sun or partial shade and in moist, very acid soil of pH 4.5 to 5.5. When transplanting, set gardenias at the depth at which they were previously growing. To keep shallow roots moist and to prevent damage that might be caused by cultivation, spread a 2-inch mulch of wood chips, sawdust or ground bark under plants. Fertilize dwarf gardenias once a month from spring through late summer with a balanced fertilizer such as 20-20-20, using 1 teaspoon for each foot of height. Prune in early spring. Remove faded flowers.

HEDGEHOG JUNIPER See *Juniperus*
HEMLOCK See *Tsuga*
HINOKI FALSE CYPRESS See *Chamaecyparis*
HOLLY See *Ilex*
HORNIBROOK AUSTRIAN PINE See *Pinus*

ILEX
I. crenata 'Dwarf Pagoda' (Dwarf Pagoda holly); *I. crenata* 'Heller' (Heller's holly); *I. crenata* 'Mariesii' (Maries' holly); *I. crenata vomitoria nana* (dwarf yaupon)

The shiny green leaves of holly can be enjoyed year round indoors by growing one of the compact evergreen dwarfs, which can be kept under 1 foot in height by pruning. They are round and squat, with fine-toothed, glossy dark green leaves. Dwarf Pagoda holly, the smallest of these varieties, has leaves ¼ inch long and inconspicuous black fruit. Unpruned, it grows less than 1 foot tall and 15 inches wide. Heller's holly has elliptical leaves ½ to 1 inch long. It will grow 1 foot high and 3 feet wide if unpruned. Maries' holly has oval leaves ¼ inch wide; it grows less than 1 inch a year. Dwarf yaupon grows into a compact round mass 1½ to 4 feet tall if unpruned. Its shiny gray-green leaves are oblong and 1 inch wide. Each of these hollies may also be grown outdoors in a mild climate.

HOW TO GROW. Dwarf hollies are hardy outdoors in Zones 7-10. They grow best in full sun or partial shade, planted in well-drained, acid soil with a pH of 5.5 to 6.5. Do not feed them until one year after planting; thereafter, fertilize them once a year in early spring with a balanced fertilizer such as 10-10-10. Keep the soil moist during the growing season but allow it to become drier in the early fall to bring the plant's new growth to maturity. A mulch of wood chips, ground bark, pine needles or peat moss will keep roots cool and moist. Transplant hollies in early spring or early fall, setting them at the same depth as they were previously growing.

Indoors, give hollies full sun, or provide very bright artificial light for 14 to 16 hours a day. Plants will prosper in temperatures between 40° and 60° at night and below 75° during the day. Protect them from hot-air drafts. Hollies are relatively free of pests and diseases.

JAPANESE CEDAR See *Cryptomeria*
JAPANESE RED PINE See *Pinus*
JAPANESE WHITE PINE See *Pinus*

JUNIPERUS
J. chinensis 'Echiniformis,' also called *J. communis* 'Echiniformis' (hedgehog juniper); *J. communis* 'Depressa' (dwarf common juniper); *J. horizontalis* 'Glomerata' (dwarf creeping juniper); *J. horizontalis* 'Wiltonii' (Wilton carpet juniper); *J. virginiana* 'Pendula Nana' (weeping dwarf red cedar)

Height 7 in. at 6 years

DWARF PAGODA HOLLY
Ilex crenata 'Dwarf Pagoda'

Small junipers, like their larger counterparts, grow as trees or shrubs—trailing, weeping, upright or creeping. The foliage of these conifers is usually spiny and sharply pointed on young plants, while on mature plants it is scalelike and very tightly pressed together. The standard Chinese juniper may grow 60 feet tall with upraised branches; the hedgehog variety, a slow-growing dwarf, becomes 1 to 2 feet high and not much wider. A good pot plant, it has a humped, almost globular shape and dark green, short, prickly needles.

The common juniper grows as a shrub or tree and may reach 35 feet. Its dwarf variety Depressa, a dense spreading shrub, will eventually cover an area 8 to 10 feet wide with trailing branches but it seldom grows more than 3 feet tall. Prickly green needles turn brownish in winter unless the shrub is grown in shade.

The standard creeping juniper is a trailing bluish-green shrub 12 to 18 inches tall; its main branches are flat but its smaller branches are erect. Glomerata is a dwarf variety 40 inches wide at 18 years, but only 6 inches high. It has long, pinkish-brown main branches and foliage that is rich green in summer, with a purple cast in winter. Wilton carpet juniper, another dwarf variety, forms a steel-blue mat seldom more than 6 inches high.

Unlike the standard red cedar, which grows slowly to 90 feet, the weeping dwarf variety seldom reaches more than 20 inches in height.

HOW TO GROW. Hedgehog juniper is hardy in Zones 4-10; common, creeping and carpet junipers and red cedars in Zones 2-9. They grow best in full sun with well-drained soil, but tolerate almost any dry location that has an acid or neutral soil. The red cedar may even grow best in poor, sandy soil. While these conifers are susceptible to few pests and diseases, the hedgehog juniper is sometimes attacked by red spider mites, the red cedar by rust, and the creeping juniper by bacterial blights. Dwarf conifers occasionally revert to their standard form by putting out a full-sized branch; when this happens, remove the branch completely.

KINGSVILLE DWARF BOXWOOD See *Buxus*

LAWSON'S FALSE CYPRESS See *Chamaecyparis*
LITTLE LEAF BOXWOOD See *Buxus*

MUGO PINE See *Pinus*
MYRTLE-LEAF ORANGE See *Citrus*

NORWAY SPRUCE See *Picea*

ORANGE See *Citrus*
ORIENTAL SPRUCE See *Picea*

PICEA
P. abies 'Nidiformis' (dwarf Norway spruce); *P. abies* 'Tabuliformis' (dwarf Norway spruce); *P. glauca* 'Albertiana Conica' (dwarf Alberta spruce); *P. orientalis* 'Nana' (dwarf Oriental spruce); *P. pungens* 'Glauca Procumbens' (dwarf Colorado blue spruce); *P. pungens* 'Montgomery' (dwarf Colorado blue spruce)

Desirable for their hardiness, compactness and fine color, these dwarf spruces grow as short, symmetrical cones and globes or as spreading plants. Diminutive as they seem in contrast to standard spruces, which may reach a height of 150 feet, the dwarf spruces are substantial specimens in small gardens. Nidiformis is a dense, spreading dull green dwarf Norway spruce that grows 3 feet tall and 5 feet wide in about 50 years. When it is young, it often has a depression in

Height 1 to 2 ft.

HEDGEHOG JUNIPER
Juniperus chinensis 'Echiniformis'

Size 1 by 10 ft. in 75 years

GRAFTED DWARF COLORADO BLUE SPRUCE
Picea pungens 'Glauca Procumbens'

For climate zones, see map, page 151.

House plants, page 123;   Orchids, page 131;   Rock garden plants, page 134;   Roses, page 143;   Vegetables and fruits, page 145.

its flat top, caused by the arching habit of the juvenile branches. Tabuliformis, another dwarf Norway spruce, may grow 3½ feet tall and 5 feet wide in 35 years. Pale green, it spreads horizontally, touching the ground with its slightly drooping branches.

The dwarf Alberta spruce may grow 10 feet tall in 40 years. Compact and cone-shaped, it grows slowly and has dense branches covered with green needles that are aromatic when crushed. Dwarf Oriental spruce is a low, globe-shaped shrub. It carries very short, irregularly spreading branches with bright green needles.

Glauca Procumbens is a dwarf Colorado blue spruce that may become 1 foot tall and 10 feet wide in 75 years. Its needles are long and gray-blue and its branches spread along the ground. When grafted onto a tall rootstock, Glauca Procumbens takes on a graceful, arching form. The Montgomery variety grows about 3 inches a year to become a compact, broadly conical dwarf.

HOW TO GROW. With one exception these dwarf varieties grow well in Zones 2-7; the dwarf Oriental spruce is hardy to Zone 4. Although full sun and moist soil are best, dwarf spruces will survive almost any exposure; Colorado blue spruces also tolerate air pollution. The Oriental species needs rich loam and a shady location in Zones 4 and 5 to prevent leaf burn in winter; Alberta spruce grows best in sandy loam.

Dwarf spruces are susceptible to red spider mites. Reversion to standard size is sometimes a problem; remove any oversized branches.

PINE See *Pinus*

PINUS
P. densiflora 'Pendula' (dwarf Japanese red pine); *P. mugo* 'Mops' (dwarf mugo pine); *P. nigra* 'Hornibrookiana' (Hornibrook Austrian pine); *P. parviflora* 'Gimborn's Pyramid' (dwarf Japanese white pine); *P. strobus* 'Umbraculifera' (dwarf eastern white pine); *P. sylvestris* 'Beauvronensis' (dwarf Scotch pine)

Dwarf pines vary in hardiness and growth habit. The standard pine species range in size up to 120 feet; dwarf pines are smaller and more appropriate for small settings. Pendula has drooping branches with light blue-green summer foliage turning pale green in winter. It grows 2 to 3 feet tall and 15 to 20 feet wide. Mops, a dwarf mugo pine, is a bushy plant that slowly grows 1 to 2 feet high and nearly as wide. Hornibrook Austrian pine is a dense dwarf with dark green foliage that reaches 2 to 3 feet in 50 years. Gimborn's Pyramid, a compact, broad, slow-growing shrub, has needles that are very blue, especially in spring.

Umbraculifera, a dwarf eastern white pine, is a compact, umbrella-shaped plant which grows 3 feet tall. It is light green and flat-topped with bending branches. The dwarf Scotch pine Beauvronensis grows very slowly to become 20 inches tall and 30 inches wide.

HOW TO GROW. Hardiness Zones for these conifers are as follows: mugo, Austrian and Scotch pines, Zones 3-7; stone pine and eastern white pine, to Zone 4; Japanese red pine and Japanese white pine, to Zone 5. All grow best when they are planted in full sun and in well-drained soil. In sandy soil, pines grow more densely and slowly. Eastern white pine does well in sandy soil but adapts to clay soil. The stone and Scotch pines will thrive in dry, rocky soil. Austrian pine needs an especially acid soil. Dwarf pines are fairly pest- and disease-resistant. Occasionally a full-sized branch may grow on a dwarf pine; if such a reversion to standard size occurs, remove the branch completely.

Height 1 to 2 ft.

DWARF MUGO PINE
Pinus mugo 'Mops'

PSEUDOTSUGA
P. menziesii 'Densa' (dwarf Douglas fir)

A dwarf Douglas fir, 3½ feet tall at most, Densa is a broad flat-topped shrub. Unlike the 250-foot Douglas fir, which achieves a broad conical shape, this small, dense plant has horizontal branches that are matted with short needles and project irregularly. Its unique shape as well as its bluish cast make it ideal as a specimen plant in a small garden. Densa can also be used as a low-growing informal or formal hedge. Shear in early spring so that new growth will hide the cuts.

HOW TO GROW. The dwarf Douglas fir grows well in Zones 4-6, thriving in full sun with moist, well-drained soil. This conifer is susceptible to the Douglas-fir pitch moth, a borer that can be controlled with an insecticide. The Douglas fir is sometimes an alternate host for pests that attack other garden plants, but careful weeding around this little shrub may protect it from infestation.

RED CEDAR See *Juniperus*

RHODODENDRON
R. forrestii repens; R. impeditum (Cloudland rhododendron); *R.* 'Keiskei' (Keisk rhododendron); *R. radicans* (Rockmantle rhododendron) (all dwarf rhododendrons); *R. kiusianum, R. kiusianum* 'Komo Kulshan'; *R. nakaharai; R. rukizon* (all dwarf azaleas)

Dwarf rhododendrons provide gardeners of the northeast and northwest United States with an abundant bouquet of bell- or funnel-shaped flowers in early spring or early summer. Dwarf azaleas lend similar cheer to the Southeast, the Gulf Coast and Southern California in late spring or summer. All are dense, compact plants, less than 12 inches tall and well suited for a miniature or rock garden.

RHODODENDRONS: *R. forrestii repens* is a creeping rhododendron that grows only 3 to 6 inches tall. Its leathery oval leaves are ½ to 2 inches long, dark green on top. Bright scarlet flowers up to 2 inches wide appear in spring. Cloudland rhododendron grows 1 to 1½ feet tall and has elliptical leaves ⅝ inch long. In the spring mauve to purple flowers bloom; they are ½ inch long and mildly fragrant. Keisk rhododendron usually grows no taller than 2½ feet; its narrow leaves, olive-green on top and brown underneath, are about 2 inches long. Pale yellow flowers about 1 inch wide bloom in early spring. Rockmantle, the smallest of rhododendrons, grows only 3 inches tall and has dark green, shiny leaves ½ inch long. In early summer it produces rose-purple to purple flowers ¾ inch long.

AZALEAS: *R. kiusianum* is a spreading evergreen shrub, usually less than 2½ feet tall; its bright green leaves are 1 inch long. Purple (rarely white or crimson) flowers 1 inch wide appear in late spring. The variety Komo Kulshan is similar but only 1½ feet high, with flowers rose-pink on the outer edge and pale pink in the center. *R. nakaharai* is the lowest growing of the azaleas, a creeping shrub less than 1 foot tall with leaves 1 inch long. Orange to dark brick-red flowers bloom in the summer. *R. rukizon,* about 1 foot tall, has waxy heart-shaped leaves ½ inch long. Salmon-orange flowers bloom in early summer.

HOW TO GROW. *R.* Keiskei and *R. impeditum* are hardy in Zones 5-10, *R. forrestii* and *R. radicans* in Zones 6-10. The azaleas are hardy in Zones 6-10. All grow best in partial shade in an acid soil with a pH 5 to 6; it should contain a large amount of organic matter. Before planting, mix the garden loam with equal parts of pea gravel or coarse sand and ground redwood or oak leaves.

Transplant rhododendrons in spring, or in fall where win-

For climate zones, see map, page 151.

Height 3½ ft.

DWARF DOUGLAS FIR
Pseudotsuga menziesii 'Densa'

Height to 6 in. Flower to 2 in. Leaf to 2 in.

DWARF RHODODENDRON
Rhododendron forrestii repens

Height 3 in. Flower ¾ in. Leaf ½ in.

DWARF RHODODENDRON
Rhododendron radicans

House plants, page 123;   Orchids, page 131;   Rock garden plants, page 134;   Roses, page 143;   Vegetables and fruits, page 145.

Height 2 to 2½ ft. Flower 1 in. Leaf 1 in.

DWARF AZALEA
Rhododendron kiusianum

Height 10 in. Flower 1½ in. Leaf 1 in.

DWARF AZALEA
Rhododendron nakaharai

Size 6 by 4½ ft. in 30 years

DWARF AMERICAN ARBORVITAE
Thuja occidentalis 'Rheingold'

ter cold will not cause damage. Set plants an inch higher in the soil than they grew at the nursery. The soil around the shallow roots must be kept cool and moist but well drained. Spread a 2-inch mulch of wood chips, ground bark, pine needles or coarse peat moss beneath the shrubs; continue to add to this mulch each year as it decomposes. Fertilize in early spring, dusting the soil with cottonseed meal or a fertilizer formulated for acid-loving plants. Apply at no more than half the strength recommended on the label. Pinch off faded blooms so the plants will flower more the following year.

SAWARA FALSE CYPRESS See *Chamaecyparis*
SCOTCH PINE See *Pinus*
SPINY WHITE CEDAR See *Chamaecyparis*
SPRUCE See *Picea*

THUJA

T. occidentalis globosa 'Tom Thumb' (dwarf American arborvitae, dwarf white cedar); *T. occidentalis* 'Hetz Midget' (dwarf American arborvitae, dwarf white cedar); *T. occidentalis* 'Rheingold' (dwarf American arborvitae, dwarf white cedar)

Dwarf varieties of the American arborvitae are usually dense and symmetrical in growth. All of them have scalelike leaves carried in flat, fan-shaped clusters on their branchlets. A 20-year-old Tom Thumb may be rounded, 4 feet tall and 5 feet wide, while its standard counterpart may have grown to a slender, conical 40 feet. Tom Thumb foliage is a light, dull green and darkens in winter.

Hetz Midget, a slow-growing dwarf, may be only 1 foot in diameter after 10 years of growth; it adds about 1½ inches a year. Its tiny crowded sprays of foliage are light green, turning slightly bronze in autumn. Rheingold may reach 6 feet tall and 4½ feet wide in 30 years; it may be globe- or cone-shaped. The spiny new foliage is soft green in summer and copper-colored in winter when it is planted in full sun. In shade, the foliage turns dull brownish green in winter. With the growth of mature scalelike foliage, the leaves become gold in winter.

HOW TO GROW. Dwarf American arborvitaes are hardy in Zones 2-8. They grow best in full sun and humid air and also need moist soil, often requiring mulching to prevent winter burn from loss of moisture. Plants may need to be sprayed to control red spider mites, juniper blight and leaf miners.

TSUGA

T. canadensis 'Cole' (dwarf Canadian hemlock); *T. canadensis* 'Jervis' (dwarf Canadian hemlock); *T. canadensis* 'Minuta' (dwarf Canadian hemlock); *T. canadensis* 'Pendula' (dwarf Canadian hemlock)

Some of the smallest conifers known are varieties of Canadian hemlock. Although the graceful standard trees with their curving branches and shining dark needles sometimes reach a height of 90 feet, the smallest varieties may grow no more than 6 inches tall. Cole is the lowest growing; unless trained upward it will grow prostrate, its main branches hugging the ground. After 25 years it may spread 40 inches wide but still stand only 6 inches high. It is an ideal plant for a rock garden.

The Jervis Canadian hemlock grows very slowly, reaching its ultimate height of 8 to 10 inches in 15 years. It has dense, short, uneven branches bearing clusters of medium-green needles about ¼ inch long. Minuta is very compact; seldom more than 10 inches tall at 25 years of age, it grows almost as broad as it is high. Pendula, a weeping dwarf Canadian hemlock, is a somewhat globular shrub when young, becoming dome-shaped in maturity. In 25 to 50 years, its hanging branches cascade from a height of 15 feet and spread to a width of about 30 feet. When young, it is attractive in a patio container, and it tolerates close shearing.

HOW TO GROW. Canadian hemlocks are hardy in Zones 4-8 where rainfall and atmospheric moisture are high and pollution levels are low. They grow best in acid, well-drained soil. Although they tolerate partial shade, full sun is best. Their foliage needs protection from exposure in cold winters when the needles may dry out. Hemlocks seldom need fertilizing, but if foliage thins or grows pale, a light dusting of the soil with cottonseed meal in spring will correct the condition. Infestations of spruce mites and black vine weevils can be treated with insecticides. Hemlocks are easy to transplant.

WHITE CEDAR See *Chamaecyparis* and *Thuja*

Ferns

ADIANTUM
A. reniforme (maidenhair fern)

One of the smallest and most delicate of the maidenhair ferns, *A. reniforme* has kidney-shaped fronds that are ¾ to 2½ inches across. These float on thin, glossy stems 4 to 9 inches long, which grow in fan-shaped clusters. Maidenhair ferns grow through the summer, forming dense clumps, then are dormant until the following spring.

HOW TO GROW. This species is somewhat difficult to grow, but is evergreen outdoors in Zones 9 and 10 if it is given a sheltered spot, partial shade and moist, slightly acid to neutral soil (pH 6.0 to 7.0). Plant in a mixture of 1 part loam, 1 part coarse sand and 2 parts leaf mold or peat moss. Add 2 tablespoons of ground limestone per cubic foot of soil. Remove yellowed fronds in fall and winter.

Indoors, these ferns need high humidity (60 per cent or more), temperatures above 60° at night and 65° during the day, and medium-bright indirect light. A woodland terrarium is ideal if it has an opening large enough to permit pruning of dead fronds. Pot in a mixture that contains equal parts of packaged potting soil, peat moss or leaf mold, and coarse sand. Add 1 teaspoon of ground limestone per quart of mix. Keep the soil moist but not soggy, and reduce watering during winter dormancy. Fertilize twice during the growing season with fish emulsion diluted to half the strength recommended on the label. Maidenhair ferns grow best when their roots crowd the container. Shriveled leaves may be caused by poor root development (the pot may be too large) or inadequate humidity. If an established clump dies from the center, cut out the dead part and fill the hole with soil. Maidenhair ferns may be propagated by division in spring.

ASPLENIUM
A. ebenoides, also known as *Asplenosorus ebenoides* and *Camptosorus ebenoides* (Scott's spleenwort); *A. trichomanes* (maidenhair spleenwort)

These ferns are ideal inhabitants for a rocky woodland garden or a terrarium. Scott's spleenwort is a naturally occurring hybrid that is not always fertile. Its 5- to 6-inch tapering fronds are extremely irregular. The lower part of the frond is cut into leaflets of differing shapes, while the upper third of the frond is usually wavy but uncut. New fronds lie flat on the ground; mature ones are more erect. Sometimes, like the walking fern (*Camptosorus rhizophyllus,* one of its parents), Scott's spleenwort will sprout a new plant at a leaf tip. The dainty maidenhair spleenwort has ¼-inch leaflets paired along dark, lustrous stalks. Its 3- to 6-inch-long sterile fronds

Size 6 by 40 in. in 25 years

DWARF CANADIAN HEMLOCK
Tsuga canadensis 'Cole'

Frond size ¾ to 2½ in. across. Stem length 4 to 9 in.

MAIDENHAIR FERN
Adiantum reniforme

For climate zones, see map, page 151.

House plants, page 123;   Orchids, page 131;   Rock garden plants, page 134;   Roses, page 143;   Vegetables and fruits, page 145.   119

Frond length 5 to 6 in.

SCOTT'S SPLEENWORT
Asplenium ebenoides

Leaf length 1/20 in.

MOSQUITO FERN
Azolla filiculoides

form rock-hugging rosettes, which are evergreen in warmer areas, while the upright fertile fronds sprout late in summer and wither in early winter.

HOW TO GROW. Scott's spleenwort is difficult to establish outdoors, but in Zones 3-8 it will grow in sheltered locations in partial or full shade. Maidenhair spleenwort is hardy in Zones 3-8. In very moist locations it withstands full sun, but it grows best in the shade. Temperatures that range from 50° at night to 75° in the daytime during spring and summer are ideal for both of these ferns; they can withstand extremes of summer heat for only a few days.

Scott's spleenwort and maidenhair spleenwort grow best when they are planted in crevices between rocks, where they are less likely to be overwhelmed by other plants. They prefer alkaline soil (pH 7.0 to 8.0) that is constantly moist but well drained. To a mixture of 1 part loam, 1 part coarse sand and 2 parts peat moss or leaf mold, add 2 tablespoons of ground limestone to each cubic foot of soil mixture. To avoid stimulating unseasonal growth, do not trim live fronds during winter dormancy.

Indoors, both ferns will thrive in the high humidity of a terrarium. Keep them cool and out of direct sun. Night temperatures should be cool, though not lower than 50°, and day temperatures 65° to 75°. Plant in a mix of equal parts of packaged potting soil, coarse sand and peat moss or leaf mold, adding 2 teaspoons of bone meal and 1 teaspoon of ground limestone to each quart of mix. Keep the soil moist but not soggy, and do not let water collect on the fronds; water less during the winter rest period. Established plants need fertilizing twice during the growing season; use fish emulsion diluted to half the strength recommended on the label. Trim dead fronds regularly, being careful not to disturb the plant's shallow roots. Propagate maidenhair spleenwort by division of the crown in spring; Scott's spleenwort may be propagated by cutting a well-rooted new fern from the tip of an old frond.

ASPLENOSORUS See *Asplenium*

AZOLLA
A. filiculoides (mosquito fern, duckweed fern)
In the wild, mosquito fern forms a dense carpet on the surface of warm, sluggish water, supposedly discouraging mosquitoes from breeding. It grows wild on the West Coast and from New York south to Florida and Texas, where its rapid growth can make it difficult to contain. The narrow, pointed leaves are less than 1/20 inch long and grow in two rows along branching stems; the stems also sprout dangling, threadlike rootlets. The leaves are red in sunlight and green in shade. In outdoor pools, mosquito fern dies in winter and renews itself from spores in the spring.

HOW TO GROW. In Zones 6-10, mosquito fern is hardy outdoors in warm (70° to 75°), still water that has a pH of 6.5 to 7.0 and contains some organic matter. It will tolerate full sun but grows best in shade.

Grow the mosquito fern indoors in an aquarium, or in a terrarium in mud or a saucer of water. The plant needs bright indirect or curtain-filtered sunlight or it will quickly weaken and die. Air temperature should range from 50° at night to 80° during the day. Propagate the mosquito fern by division, cutting off rooted sections and floating them on the surface of the water.

CAMPTOSORUS See *Asplenium*

DUCKWEED FERN See *Azolla*

Bulbs, page 98;   Cacti and succulents, page 105;   Evergreens, page 110;   Ferns, page 119;   Grasses, shrubs and trees, page 121;

LEMMAPHYLLUM

L. microphyllum

The succulent fronds of this tiny fern do not conform to the popular image of a fernlike frond, and its thin, creeping stem often behaves like a vine. Seldom planted outdoors, it has very narrow uncut spore-bearing fronds 1 to 2 inches long, while the sterile ones are oval and only half as long.

HOW TO GROW. Slow-growing *L. microphyllum* is well suited to an indoor life in a pot or terrarium, or it can be grown on a pole of tree fern or osmunda fiber. Place it in bright indirect or curtain-filtered sunlight, at temperatures ranging from 50° to 60° at night and from 70° to 80° during the day. Provide at least 60 per cent humidity. For a pot or terrarium, use a well-drained mixture of 1 part leaf mold or peat moss, 1 part builder's sand and 2 parts perlite or vermiculite; for each gallon of this mix add 2 tablespoons of bone meal. Terrarium plants may be kept smaller by withholding additional fertilizer; established potted plants need to be fertilized twice during the spring and summer with fish emulsion diluted to half the recommended strength. Plants grown on tree fern or osmunda need to be fertilized once a month. Newly potted or repotted ferns should not be fertilized for six months. Propagate by stem division.

MAIDENHAIR FERN See *Adiantum*
MAIDENHAIR SPLEENWORT See *Asplenium*
MOSQUITO FERN See *Azolla*

OAK FERN See *Quercifilix*

QUERCIFILIX

Q. zeilancia, also called *Tectaria zeilanica* (oak fern)

A little-known fern that is native to southern Asia from Sri Lanka to Taiwan, the delicate oak fern makes a delightful addition to a woodland terrarium. The plant bears two kinds of fronds on its thin, creeping stems. The lobed sterile fronds resemble oak leaves and are 2 to 6 inches long and ¾ to 2 inches wide. The fertile fronds are stalklike and from 5 to 9 inches long.

HOW TO GROW. Oak ferns grow best in a covered container because they need high humidity, at least 60 per cent. Plant in a mixture of 1 part garden loam, 1 part builder's sand and 2 parts leaf mold or peat moss. A combination of equal parts of vermiculite and perlite may be used instead of the builder's sand. Keep the soil moist but not soggy, and place the container in a room where temperatures do not fall below 60° at night or below 65° in the daytime. Provide indirect or filtered light, or artificial light of medium intensity. Propagate by dividing the crown.

SCOTT'S SPLEENWORT See *Asplenium*

TECTARIA See *Quercifilix*

Grasses, shrubs and trees

ACER

A. palmatum 'dissectum' (threadleaf Japanese maple)

With its gnarled, pendulous branches and lacy leaves, the threadleaf Japanese maple is an outstanding specimen tree to use as a focal point in the garden, to grow as a tub plant or to train as a bonsai. The deeply cut fan-shaped leaves are bronze-red in spring, reddish green in summer and crimson in autumn. The slow-growing Japanese threadleaf maple takes 20 years or more to form spreading mounds up to 6 feet tall and 9 feet or more in width.

For climate zones, see map, page 151.

Frond length 1 to 2 in.

Lemmaphyllum microphyllum

Sterile frond length 2 to 6 in. Fertile frond length 5 to 9 in.

OAK FERN
Quercifilix zeilanica

THREADLEAF JAPANESE MAPLE
Acer palmatum 'Dissectum'

Size 6 by 9 ft.

DWARF BAMBOO
Arundinaria pygmaea

Height 10 in. Leaf to 5 in.

HOW TO GROW. Hardy outdoors in Zones 5-10, the thread-leaf Japanese maple grows best where it receives full sun for part of the morning and afternoon but is shaded during the hottest part of the day. It may also be grown where it is in dappled shade all day, but its leaf color will not be as intense. Well-drained garden loam enriched with organic matter such as peat moss or compost is ideal. A slightly acid to neutral pH of 6.0 to 7.0 is recommended. Fertilize in spring with a balanced fertilizer such as 10-10-10 following label recommendations. If late spring frosts damage foliage, prune away dead branches when growth begins again. Thinning branches periodically from the center of the tree reveals its attractive form and also improves air circulation.

To grow these maples in containers, pot in a soil mixture composed of equal parts of garden loam and peat moss. Fertilize once a year in the spring with 10-10-10 fertilizer. Keep well watered during spring through fall; during winter, water only if the soil feels completely dry to the touch. Winter temperatures of 35° to 45° at night and temperatures of 55° to 60° in the daytime are best; in northernmost zones, move container-grown plants to protected areas or mulch them and wrap them in burlap.

ARUNDINARIA

A. pygmaea, also known as *Sasa pygmaea* (dwarf bamboo or pygmy bamboo)

The tiny, bright green canes of dwarf bamboo are $1/16$ inch in diameter and only 10 inches tall. Growing from short stalks, the leaves taper from ¾-inch bases to sharp points and are up to 5 inches long; they are brilliant green on top, gray-green underneath, and covered with fine hairs. A fast-spreading ground cover in a mild climate, dwarf bamboo can also be grown in a pot.

HOW TO GROW. Dwarf bamboo can be grown indoors in a container, using any good potting soil with a pH of 6.5. Put a layer of coarse gravel in the bottom of the container to ensure good drainage. Place the container in bright indirect light. Keep the soil moist and fertilize monthly with a balanced fertilizer such as 10-10-10 diluted to half the strength recommended on the label. If the leaves become pale, fertilize with a high-nitrogen fertilizer such as 20-10-10. Outdoors, dwarf bamboo thrives in Zones 8-10 in any slightly acid, fertile well-drained soil and in partial shade. Plant bamboo outdoors in early spring in the Gulf states, in late spring elsewhere; the soil should be warm. Set plants at the depth at which they were already growing; the canes turn from green to white at the soil line. Keep roots moist and mulch with leaf mold. Bamboo spreads rapidly; to confine it, set a shield of fine copper screening or aluminum or stainless steel 1 foot into the ground around the plot.

Fertilize once every other year if the bamboo is growing in rich soil, every year if it is in poor soil; scatter dried manure or cottonseed meal on top of the soil. Propagate by dividing the rhizomes in early spring before new growth appears.

BAMBOO See *Arundinaria*

DEPRESSED WILLOW See *Salix*

EQUISETUM

E. scirpoides (dwarf scouring rush, horsetail)

The dwarf scouring rush is a plant for a wet environment. It is small in stature but spreads rapidly by underground stems unless it is confined in a container. Thus restrained, it is useful as a low accent plant in front of a larger plant. The evergreen stems of the dwarf scouring rush either form curling, tangled mats or grow rigidly upright, but they seldom grow longer than 6 inches.

HOW TO GROW. This dwarf is hardy in Zones 3-8. Outdoors it grows best in full sun and wet, moderately acid soil. A small clump can be planted in a pot and the pot sunk in the earth or set in shallow water.

Indoors, give the dwarf scouring rush direct sun or bright artificial light for 14 to 16 hours a day. Temperatures of 45° to 50° at night and 65° to 75° in daytime and a humidity of 60 per cent are ideal. Plant in equal parts of commercial potting soil, coarse sand and peat moss, with a teaspoon of bone meal added to each quart of the mixture. In spring and summer, fertilize twice with fish emulsion diluted to half the strength recommended on the label. Submerge the pot to half its depth in a decorative container of water, or let it stand in a saucer of water.

HORSETAIL See *Equisetum*

JAPANESE MAPLE See *Acer*

MAPLE See *Acer*

NEATLEAF WILLOW See *Salix*

PYGMY BAMBOO See *Arundinaria*

SALIX
S. reticulata (depressed willow, neatleaf willow)
Growing among small rocks, the depressed willow, a creeping dwarf, spreads a dense cover of round, dark green leaves that are whitish underneath and ½ to 1 inch long. The mat grows only 3 to 6 inches high. In early summer, after the leaves appear, catkins ½ inch long rise on long slender stalks from the dense foliage. The plant grows in mountainous regions from Arctic Alaska south to Colorado. It is especially appropriate for a rock garden.

HOW TO GROW. Depressed willow grows in Zones 3 and 4 where the climate resembles that of its native habitat: cool temperatures without extreme summer heat; full sun or partial shade; abundant water to keep soil moist but not soggy; and a rock cleft to hold the roots. Propagate by division, cutting and separating the creeping stems.

SASA See *Arundinaria*
SCOURING RUSH See *Equisetum*

THREADLEAF JAPANESE MAPLE See *Acer*

House plants
AFRICAN VIOLETS See *Saintpaulia*
ALUMINUM PLANT See *Pilea*

BABY'S TEARS See *Soleirolia*

BEGONIA
B. bogneri (grass-leaf begonia, grass begonia); *B. bowerae* 'Nigramarga'; *B. prismatocarpa*; *B.* 'China Doll'; *B.* 'Bebe'
Excellent candidates for a terrarium or window sill, these tiny begonias are grown for the varied patterns of their foliage as well as for their flowers. The tuberous grass-leaf begonia has unusual 5-inch-long grasslike leaves and bears four-petaled pink flowers throughout the year. The other begonias listed are rhizomatous types with horizontal succulent stems. Outlined with fine white hairs and marked with

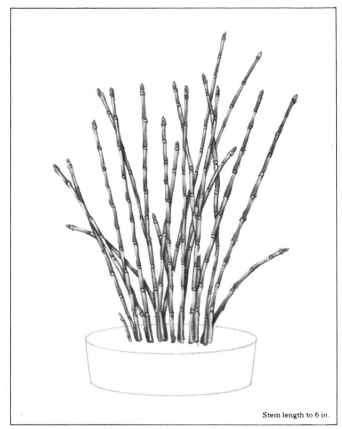

Stem length to 6 in.

DWARF SCOURING RUSH
Equisetum scirpoides

Height 7 in. Flower ½ in. Spread 3 to 6 in.

DEPRESSED WILLOW
Salix reticulata

For climate zones, see map, page 151.

House plants, page 123;   Orchids, page 131;   Rock garden plants, page 134;   Roses, page 143;   Vegetables and fruits, page 145.

black, the mint-green leaves of Nigramarga are ¾ inch wide; light pink flowers bloom in winter. *B. prismatocarpa* has shiny apple-green leaves and bright yellow flowers that are almost always in bloom. China Doll produces pink flowers in winter and spring; its 1-inch leaves are irregularly patterned in light green and purplish brown. Bebe also blooms in winter and spring, bearing clusters of white flowers above 1½-inch tapered leaves with red stems.

HOW TO GROW. Nigramarga, China Doll and Bebe do best with temperatures of 60° to 65° at night, and 68° to 72° by day, and a humidity of about 50 per cent. Set the pots in pebble-filled trays; keep the pebbles moist but be sure the water line remains below the bottom of the pots. During the winter these begonias will thrive in east, west and south windows if they receive four hours of direct sunlight a day; for the rest of the year they need to be shielded from direct sunlight. Grass-leaf begonia and *B. prismatocarpa* should be grown in terrariums where the humidity is 60 to 70 per cent. Place the terrarium where it will receive bright indirect light. Begonias also grow well under artificial light. Give a tuberous variety 12 to 14 hours a day of medium light. To flower, winter-blooming rhizomatous types should receive only 8 to 10 hours of light a day, beginning in September; at the same time lower night temperatures about 20° to simulate the natural seasonal change. Then gradually increase light to 12 to 14 hours per day.

All of these begonias may be planted in a packaged potting mix for African violets, though grass-leaf begonia and *B. prismatocarpa* do best when they are planted in milled sphagnum moss. Rhizomatous begonias store food and water in their fleshy stems, so let the soil dry slightly between waterings; tuberous begonia roots should be kept evenly moist but never soggy. Fertilize established plants every three or four weeks during the growing season with houseplant fertilizer diluted to one-quarter strength. To propagate, separate tubers or divide rhizomes in early spring. Stem or leaf cuttings may be rooted at any time in a moist mixture of equal parts of vermiculite and perlite.

BLACK-LEAF PANAMIGA See *Pilea*
BLUE TROLL BROWALLIA See *Browallia*

BROWALLIA

B. speciosa major 'Blue Troll' (Blue Troll browallia)

A compact ball of dark green foliage covered with tiny five-petaled flowers, Blue Troll browallia is a miniature that grows only 6 inches tall, less than half the height of standard varieties. Its velvety symmetrical flowers are 1 inch wide and bloom profusely from spring until frost in the garden and all year round indoors. Because of its compact shape and slow growth, this miniature can be grown in a 3-inch pot; outdoors it is a good choice for a miniature landscape.

HOW TO GROW. Indoors, Blue Troll needs at least four hours of direct sunlight a day from fall through winter. For the rest of the year provide bright indirect or curtain-filtered sunlight so the plant will have steady light but no direct rays. Maintain temperatures of 55° to 60° at night and 68° to 72° in the daytime. Sow seeds indoors for blooms 18 to 20 weeks later. When seedlings are 2 to 3 inches tall, pot them in a mixture of 2 parts peat moss to 1 part commercial potting soil and 1 part coarse sand. Keep the medium evenly moist but not soggy, and fertilize plants with a standard house-plant fertilizer at one half the strength recommended on the label every two weeks during the growing season; in winter reduce feeding to once a month. Propagate additional plants from stem cuttings in late summer.

Leaf length 5 in. Flower width ⅝ in.

GRASS-LEAF BEGONIA
Begonia bogneri

Height 6 in. Flower width 1 in.

BLUE TROLL BROWALLIA
Browallia speciosa major 'Blue Troll'

Outdoors, plant Blue Troll browallia in moderately rich garden soil where it will have full sun except during the hottest hours of the day. For summer flowers, sow seeds indoors six to eight weeks before the last spring frost is due. When night temperatures remain above 50°, set out seedlings spaced 4 to 6 inches apart. Blue Troll will bloom about 16 weeks after seeds are sown. To keep the plants compact, pinch them back. To take garden plants indoors for winter bloom, dig them four to six weeks before the first fall frost is due, put them in pots and cut them back severely.

CAPE BEAUTY See *Streptocarpus*
CAPE PRIMROSE See *Streptocarpus*
CLIMBING FIG See *Ficus*
CREEPING FIG See *Ficus*

ENGLISH IVY See *Hedera*

EPISCIA
E. dianthiflora (flame violet, lace-flower vine)

The flame violet has smaller leaves and stems than those of other episcia species, but the flowers are standard-sized. A gesneriad, it is a native of tropical climates and therefore needs warmth and high humidity. Its plushlike green 1½-inch leaves form mounds up to 4 inches tall. From early spring to early fall it bears attractive pure white 1¼-inch flower tubes that have fringed edges. New plantlets develop at the tips of the runners that trail from hanging baskets or spread in terrariums.

HOW TO GROW. Flame violets grow best where they receive bright, indirect light for 14 to 16 hours a day. Temperatures ranging from 65° or more at night to 75° or more by day and humidity as close to 50 per cent as possible are ideal. Shallow rooted, they do not need deep pots. Plant them in commercial African-violet potting soil or in a soilless mixture of 1 part perlite, 1 part vermiculite and 2 parts sphagnum peat moss. Add 1 teaspoon of ground limestone to each quart of the growing medium. Keep the medium moist but not soggy and avoid getting water on the leaves. Fertilize during the growing season with a balanced house-plant fertilizer such as 20-20-20 diluted to one fourth the strength recommended on the label. Apply the diluted fertilizer for three consecutive waterings; for the fourth watering use plain water to flush away any built-up fertilizer salts, then resume regular fertilizing.

To propagate additional plants, root stem cuttings or plantlets cut from the runners in moist sand or in equal parts of moist vermiculite and perlite.

FICUS
F. pumila 'Minima,' also called *F. repens* 'Minima' (miniature climbing fig, creeping fig)

The tiny heart-shaped leaves of the Minima climbing fig, which are ½ inch long or less, are borne in pairs on slender stems that cling with aerial roots to rock, wire or wicker surfaces. When it is grown on a rock lodged in a pot, the vine forms a lacy design.

HOW TO GROW. Indoors, this vine grows best in a soilless mixture of 2 parts sphagnum peat moss, 1 part perlite and 1 part vermiculite. To each quart of mix add 1 teaspoon of ground limestone or ¼ cup of crushed egg shell. Keep this mixture constantly damp but not wet; this plant does not tolerate overwatering. Fertilize weekly with a house-plant fertilizer such as 20-20-20 diluted to one fourth the strength recommended on the label.

Climbing fig can be grown outdoors in Zones 9 and 10. It

For climate zones, see map, page 151.

Mounds to 4 in. Leaf size 1½ in. Flower length 1¼ in.

FLAME VIOLET
Episcia dianthiflora

Leaf length to ½ in.

MINIATURE CLIMBING FIG
Ficus pumila 'Minima'

Leaf length to 1½ in.

DWARF SILVER-VEINED FITTONIA
Fittonia vershafeltii argyroneura 'Minima'

Leaf length to 6 in. Flower length 1½ in.

Gesneria christii

thrives in rich soil and cool shade but will not tolerate frost. This vine is generally insect free. To propagate additional plants, cuttings may be successfully rooted in moist vermiculite at any time of the year.

FIG See *Ficus*
FISH GERANIUM See *Pelargonium*

FITTONIA
F. vershafeltii argyroneura 'Minima' (dwarf silver-veined fittonia, nerve plant)

The chalk-white veins of the dwarf silver-veined fittonia draw a second look; they are the plant's prime attraction as a miniature ornamental. The oval leaves, an inch to 1½ inches long, grow compactly in a bottle garden or terrarium where the humidity can be kept high.

HOW TO GROW. Miniature fittonia grows best indoors with a northern exposure and temperatures between 65° and 80°. Maintain humidity at about 40 per cent. Plant in equal parts of an African-violet soil mixture, peat moss and coarse sand. Keep the medium moist but not soggy; fittonia is susceptible to root rot. If spider mites appear, spray with a miticide. Whiteflies and thrips require a dusting with malathion powder. Propagate additional plants by rooting stem cuttings that include nodes, or joints, placing them in water or moist vermiculite in spring. Because the plant has a shallow root system, it is easy to transplant.

FLAME VIOLET See *Episcia*

GERANIUM See *Pelargonium*

GESNERIA
G. christii; G. cuneifolia; G. cuneifolia 'Quebradillas' (all called gesneria)

Gesnerias frequently reward an indoor gardener with continuous flowering under artificial light. These small, exotic shrubs, which may reach a height of 6 to 8 inches, can be grown in pots or terrariums. *G. christii* forms a flat rosette of 6-inch glossy, wavy leaves and produces tubular orange-red flowers 1½ inches long. *G. cuneifolia* has brilliant red tubular flowers 1½ inches long, and its dark, glossy leaves form a rosette 6 inches wide. The orange-yellow flowers of Quebradillas are 1 inch in length. Like *G. cuneifolia,* its leaves grow in a rosette. These plants, because of their leaf sizes and growth habits, may require all of the space that is available in a terrarium.

HOW TO GROW. Gesnerias bloom best in medium artificial light for 12 to 14 hours a day; they may also be grown in indirect or filtered sunlight. Keep temperatures above 65° at night and between 75° and 80° during the day. Humidity needs to be very high for best growth, from 70 to 80 per cent. Plant gesnerias in a packaged African-violet mix or in a soilless mixture of 2 parts sphagnum moss to 1 part perlite and 1 part vermiculite. Add 1 teaspoon of ground limestone to each quart of either mix.

Fertilize weekly after watering, with a balanced fertilizer such as 20-20-20 at one quarter the strength recommended on the label. The planting mix should be kept moist but not soggy; never let the soil dry out. Propagate gesneria from seeds or by separating small plants at the base, using a moist mixture of equal parts of perlite and vermiculite.

GLOXINIA See *Sinningia*
GRASS BEGONIA See *Begonia*
GRASS-LEAF BEGONIA See *Begonia*

HEDERA
H. helix 'Jubilee'; *H. helix* 'Merion Beauty'; *H. helix* 'Needlepoint'; *H. helix* 'Pixie' (all called miniature English ivy)

These elegant miniatures resemble the larger English ivy, but while the leaves of the standard plant grow 2 to 4 inches long, these varieties have leaves less than half that size. Although most of them branch, they need only a few square inches of space indoors; they are not fast growers. Each thrives in a dish garden, bottle garden or in a pot at the base of a larger plant. Jubilee has blunt-tipped variegated leaves ½ to 1 inch long, edged or marbled with creamy white, yellow or silver gray. Merion Beauty has leaves that are less than 1 inch long. It grows more rapidly than the other miniatures in this group.

Needlepoint has 1-inch leaves with five deeply cut lobes. Pixie has leaves varying from ¼ inch long up to 1¼ inches; they have five to seven lobes and grow either clustered or lapped along the stem like shingles.

HOW TO GROW. Indoors these miniatures grow best in bright indirect light or filtered sunlight. Keep night temperatures between 45° and 55° and day temperatures at 70° or lower. Maintain humidity of 50 to 60 per cent. Plant in a mixture of 2 parts potting soil and 1 part fine perlite. Keep the medium moist but not soggy, being careful not to let it become dry in winter. Fertilize the plants every two weeks in summer and once a month from fall through spring with a balanced house-plant fertilizer such as 20-20-20. Since Jubilee may lose its variegated color if it is heavily fertilized, dilute the fertilizer to one half the strength recommended on the label. Overfertilizing any of these miniatures may cause them to produce standard-sized leaves. Pests such as red spider mites and aphids can be avoided by regularly showering both sides of the foliage with water. Infested plants should be rinsed daily.

Outdoors these miniature English ivies are hardy in Zones 6-9. They grow best in filtered sunlight and moderately fertile well-drained garden soil enriched with humus. Propagate additional plants by rooting cuttings in water. A branch will also root if it is in contact with the soil; use a florist's pin to hold it in place.

HELXINE See *Soleirolia*
HORSESHOE GERANIUM See *Pelargonium*

IVY See *Hedera*
IVY GERANIUM See *Pelargonium*

KOELLIKERIA
K. erinoides (koellikeria)

A long-blooming gesneriad for a terrarium, this koellikeria bears small tubular flowers in sprays on 6- to 12-inch stalks that thrust above the low foliage. The plant grows from spreading, fleshy underground stems called rhizomes. It has oval leaves dotted with silver, 1 to 4 inches long and covered with very fine hairs.

HOW TO GROW. Give koellikeria bright indirect or curtain-filtered sunlight, or keep it 6 inches below a two-tube fluorescent fixture for 14 to 16 hours a day. Temperatures of 65° at night and 70° to 75° in the daytime are ideal, with humidity 60 per cent or more. In a terrarium at least 8 inches across and 12 inches high, set the rhizome horizontally ½ inch deep in a soilless mix of 2 parts sphagnum peat moss, 1 part vermiculite and 1 part perlite. Add 1 teaspoon of ground limestone to each quart of mix.

Water very sparingly until growth appears, then keep the mix only slightly moist. Excessive moisture will rot the bot-

Leaf length ½ to 1 in.

MINIATURE ENGLISH IVY
Hedera helix 'Jubilee'

Leaf length 1 in.

MINIATURE ENGLISH IVY
Hedera helix 'Merion Beauty'

Leaf length 1 to 4 in. Flower stalk length to 12 in.

Koellikeria erinoides

For climate zones, see map, page 151.

Height 2 to 4 in. Flower 1 in. Leaf ¾ in.

MINIATURE COMMON GERANIUM
Pelargonium hortorum
'Black Vesuvius'

Height 6 in. Flower 1 in. Leaf 1 in.

MINIATURE IVY GERANIUM
Pelargonium peltatum
'Sugar Baby'

Height 5 to 6 in. Leaf 1½ to 2 in.

DWARF ALUMINUM PLANT
Pilea cadierei 'Minima'

tom leaves. Fertilize once or twice during each growing season with a balanced water-soluble fertilizer such as 20-20-20. After the plant stops flowering, reduce watering; when all the foliage has turned yellow, cut it off. Once again, water very sparingly until growth resumes. Propagate additional plants by dividing the rhizomes or taking leaf cuttings and planting them in a moist mixture composed of equal parts of perlite and vermiculite.

LACE-FLOWER VINE See *Episcia*

NERVE PLANT See *Fittonia*

PELARGONIUM

P. hortorum varieties (miniature and dwarf zonal or common geranium, also called horseshoe or fish geranium): *P. peltatum* varieties (miniature ivy geranium)

Small geraniums thrive in pots indoors and some make fine bonsai. Outdoors, they can be used as border plants. Miniature varieties of zonal geraniums (whose round leaves are marked with horseshoe-shaped zones of white, yellow, red or brown) range from 2 to 5 inches tall, while dwarf varieties grow from 6 to 8 inches tall. Both bear globelike clusters of flowers from late winter until the following fall. Two of the smallest geraniums are the 5-inch-tall Imp, which bears salmon-pink single flowers, and the 2- to 4-inch-tall Black Vesuvius, with orange-scarlet flowers and black-zoned dark green foliage. Excellent varieties include Heidi, a miniature with pink and white double flowers, and Medley, a dwarf, with semidouble pink-veined white flowers.

Miniature ivy geraniums, which are named for their ivy-shaped leaves and vinelike stems, grow up to 6 inches tall and spread 6 to 10 inches in diameter. They bloom from late spring through fall. Sugar Baby bears bright pink flowers, while Gay Baby has single lavender flowers. These plants are attractive planted in miniature landscapes, window boxes or hanging pots.

HOW TO GROW. Indoors, geraniums need plenty of light, with cool temperatures and excellent drainage. Give them at least six hours of direct sun a day, or 14 to 16 hours of very bright artificial light. They prefer temperatures around 60° at night and no more than about 75° during the day, although they will tolerate night temperatures up to 65°. Pot the plants in well-drained commercial potting soil that is slightly acid; let the soil become moderately dry between thorough waterings. (A geranium trained as a bonsai, however, may need daily watering.) Feed plants with a house-plant fertilizer, at half the strength recommended on the label, every two weeks during the growing and flowering season, monthly the rest of the year.

Outdoors, geraniums are hardy perennials in Zones 9 and 10, but in frost zones they must be treated as tender annuals. They need full sun, or partial shade where they will have sun at least half the day, and medium-rich well-drained garden soil. Geraniums bought in bud may be set out after the danger of frost is past; space them 12 inches apart. For a flowering ground cover, space ivy geraniums 12 to 18 inches apart and pin down the stems with wire. Garden geraniums potted in the fall and moved indoors for winter flowers should be cut back severely after potting to promote vigorous growth. Propagate both zonal and ivy miniatures and dwarfs from stem cuttings at any time.

PILEA

P. cadierei 'Minima' (dwarf aluminum plant); *P. depressa; P. repens* (black-leaf panamiga) (all called pilea)

Tropical evergreens that grow no taller than 8 inches, these three types of pilea have attractive foliage and inconspicuous greenish-white or white flowers. Requiring only a modest amount of light and a 4-inch pot, they are easy to care for indoors. The dwarf aluminum plant grows only 5 or 6 inches tall; its dark green oval leaves are puffy and deeply furrowed, appearing quilted, and are streaked with bands of silver. *P. depressa* grows less than 8 inches tall and is creeping in habit, with oval leaves 1½ inches long that are scalloped near the tip. Black-leaf panamiga grows 4 to 8 inches tall; its 1¼-inch oval leaves are copper-colored on top and purple underneath.

HOW TO GROW. Pileas grow best when the temperature is kept between 65° and 70° at night and 75° and 85° during the day. Set plants on a moisture tray to keep humidity as near 50 per cent as possible. Give them indirect light, or provide moderately bright artificial light for 14 to 16 hours a day. Plant pileas in a mixture of 2 parts peat moss to 1 part potting soil and 1 part builder's sand, adding 1 teaspoon of ground limestone to each quart of the mixture. Keep the soil evenly moist but not soggy the year round. Withhold fertilizer for three or four months after potting new plants; then fertilize them every other month with a standard house-plant fertilizer diluted to half the strength recommended on the label. Propagate additional plants in spring by division or by taking stem cuttings.

SAINTPAULIA
S. hybrids (miniature African violets)

As diminutive as they are, miniature African violets nevertheless bloom in as wide a range of flower colors as their larger counterparts. And although the flowers are less than 1 inch wide, as many as 20 may bloom at once above a circle of foliage that does not exceed 6 inches in diameter. Almost any space can accommodate a collection of these bright and varied little plants in tiny pots.

Little Rascal has dark leaves and double medium blue flowers, sometimes splashed with pink or outlined in white. Mini Fantasy has leaves that are pointed and small, and profusely blooming semidouble flowers that are lavender with purple and pink dots or splashes. Pip Squeak may be the smallest African violet; its bell-shaped pink flowers and its deep green leaves are both ¼ inch long. Twinkle Toes has glossy dark leaves surrounding semidouble red blooms with white petal tips. The tiny Wee Lass, which has white double flowers with red edges, has long, narrow holly-like foliage with fluted edges.

HOW TO GROW. Miniature African violets grow best under strong artificial light for 12 hours a day in winter and 16 hours a day in summer. They also thrive in bright, curtain-filtered, indirect sunlight. On a window sill, the plants should be rotated a quarter turn every two or three days to keep their shape symmetrical and their leaves flat. Miniature African violets flower best in 60 to 75 per cent humidity with night temperatures of 60° to 65° and day temperatures 75° or higher. If a plant fails to form flower buds, removing the outer ring of leaves will stimulate flowering.

Plant these miniatures in a packaged potting soil prepared especially for African violets. Keep it barely damp, using tepid water, and fertilize monthly with a high-phosphorus formula such as 12-36-14 compounded especially for African violets. Apply the fertilizer at the strength that is recommended on the label.

Be careful not to let the soil dry out in the small pots. If the plants are in a terrarium, leave the top slightly open for ventilation. Overwatering may cause terrarium plants to de-

Rosette diameter to 6 in. Leaf 1¼ in. Flower to 1 in.

MINIATURE AFRICAN VIOLET
Saintpaulia 'Little Rascal'

For climate zones, see map, page 151.

Rosette diameter 1½ in. Flower ½ in.

MINIATURE SINNINGIA
Sinningia pusilla

Rosette diameter 1½ in. Flower ½ in.

MINIATURE SINNINGIA
Sinningia pusilla 'White Sprite'

velop crown rot. Propagate additional plants from leaf cuttings or crown divisions.

SILVER-VEINED FITTONIA See *Fittonia*

SINNINGIA
S. concinna, S. concinna hybrids; *S. pusilla; S. pusilla* 'Dollbaby' (all called miniature sinningias, miniature gloxinias)

Sturdy miniature sinningias are easily grown from tiny tubers. They have velvety leaves and tubular flowers of white or shades of red or purple. They bloom continuously under controlled fluorescent light.

S. concinna is a tiny plant whose leaves grow in a rosette 1½ inches in diameter; its ¾-inch-long flowers have white and purple petals and a purple-spotted throat. The variety Bright Eyes has delicately veined leaves and ¾-inch flowers that are purple with darker stripes. Cindy-Ella grows as a flat rosette up to 5 inches wide and bears 2-inch slipper-shaped white and purple blooms with purple-spotted throats. Freckles is an unusually profuse bloomer. When it is young it has soft, hairy olive-green leaves ½ to 1 inch long growing in rosettes. White and purple flowers with purple-spotted throats are borne on stalks 1 to 1½ inches high. Tinkerbells, which has foliage like that of Freckles, has brilliant rose-purple flowers on 6-inch trailing stalks. These four hybrids are all sterile.

The species *S. pusilla* has a 1½-inch-wide flat rosette of leaves and tubular lavender flowers ½ inch long. White Sprite, a white-flowered form of the species, has olive-green leaves. Dollbaby, a sterile hybrid, has heart-shaped leaves and 1½-inch flowers of lavender-blue with white stripes in the throats. All of these miniature sinningias grow best in terrariums, bottles or containers with high sides to retain humidity. Cindy-Ella and Dollbaby may also be grown on a sunny window sill

HOW TO GROW. Miniature sinningias flower continuously under 12 to 16 hours of artificial light daily; they also grow well in indirect filtered sunlight. Their containers must be turned every three to four days to preserve their symmetry. Keep temperatures between 65° and 70° at night and between 75° and 85° during the day. All of these miniatures need humidity of 50 to 70 per cent to grow well. Trim off dead leaves and flower stalks with small scissors; do not pull them off lest you uproot the plant.

Plant small, leafless tubers so the tops are ⅛ inch under the surface of a moist packaged African-violet mix or a soilless mixture of equal parts sphagnum peat moss, vermiculite and sharp sand or perlite. Fertilize plants growing in African-violet mix monthly with a balanced fertilizer such as 20-20-20 diluted to one half the strength recommended on the label. For plants growing in a soilless mix, fertilize for three consecutive waterings, diluting the balanced fertilizer to one fourth the strength recommended on the label. For the fourth watering, use clear water only, then resume fertilizing at the next watering. Place window-sill plants on humidifying trays to keep them from drying. Propagate additional plants by crown division; *S. concinna, S. pusilla* and White Sprite may also be propagated from seed.

SOLEIROLIA
S. soleirolii, also called *Helxine soleirolii* (baby's tears)

Modest little baby's tears is usually grown indoors, where its ground-hugging leaves make it a perfect complement to flashier plants in your terrarium or dish garden. But in Zone 10 and parts of Zones 8 and 9, it can be grown as a ground cover outdoors if it is given plenty of moisture, filtered sunlight and well-drained soil. This tiny plant, the only species of its genus, grows from fragile creeping runners that are almost translucent. The bright green oval leaves vary from ⅛ to ¼ inch in width and form a mat about 2 inches high. In the summer, inconspicuous greenish-white flowers bloom in the leaf axils.

HOW TO GROW. Baby's tears grows best in a mixture composed of equal parts of vermiculite, sand, peat moss and packaged potting soil. Keep the soil constantly moist but never soggy. The best temperature range for baby's tears is 60° to 72°, with humidity between 40 and 60 per cent. The plant will tolerate greater warmth in moist atmospheres but will lose color if the humidity falls too low. It can be propagated easily from cuttings.

STREPTOCARPUS
S. 'Cape Beauty'; *S. kirkii; S. rimicola; S. variabilis* (all called Cape primrose)

A spectacular addition to your miniature-plant collection, Cape primroses bear trumpet-shaped flowers that range from white to pink, blue or red—often with throats of deeper hues—above heavily textured stalkless leaves. The narrow deep green leaves of the Cape Beauty have purple undersides, while its pink 1-inch flowers are candy-striped with magenta. *S. kirkii* carries slipper-shaped, pale lilac flowers on 2-inch stalks above hairy round leaves 1 inch across. *S. rimicola* is an unusual one-leaved terrarium plant that dies after flowering but is easily grown from the abundant seeds it produces. Its white flowers are ¼ to ½ inch long. *S. variabilis* produces an abundance of deep blue and white flowers ¼ to ⅓ inch long. Its rounded, 1½- to 2-inch-long leaves form a compact rosette.

HOW TO GROW. Cape primroses grow best in temperatures from 50° to 65° at night and 65° to 75° by day. Since Cape Beauty, *S. rimicola* and *S. variabilis* require humidity of 60 to 70 per cent, they are best grown in a terrarium. *S. kirkii* does well with humidity ranging from 40 to 50 per cent and can be grown in an east or west window in spring and summer, a south-facing window in winter. The other Cape primroses are best grown under 12 to 14 hours a day of artificial light. Cape primroses need well-aerated soil. Use a packaged African-violet mix or a soilless mixture made of equal parts of sphagnum peat moss, vermiculite and perlite, adding 1 teaspoon of ground limestone per quart of mix. The growing medium should always be slightly moist but never soggy. Be very careful not to overwater. Fertilize all these Cape primroses except *S. variabilis* once a month during the growing season with a house-plant fertilizer diluted to one quarter the strength recommended on the label. *S. variabilis* should not be fertilized, since it is easily burned. Propagate these plants from seed. Cape Beauty can also be propagated from leaf cuttings and *S. kirkii* from stem cuttings.

Orchids

ANGRAECUM See *Neofinetia*

CATTLEYA
C. walkerana (dwarf cattleya orchid)

An exotic focal point for a small indoor garden, the dwarf cattleya orchid produces 4½-inch rose-to-lavender flowers, usually borne on short leafless shoots. The plant is unique among cattleya orchids because its flowers grow not from the tip of the pseudobulb but from near its base. One thick, oblong evergreen leaf 4 to 5 inches long accompanies each stout pseudobulb of the same length. Alternating with these

For climate zones, see map, page 151.

Height 2 in. Leaf width ⅛ to ¼ in.

BABY'S TEARS
Soleirolia soleirolii

Flower length 1 in. Leaf to 5 in.

CAPE PRIMROSE
Streptocarpus 'Cape Beauty'

Height 5 in. Flower 4½ in.

DWARF CATTLEYA ORCHID
Cattleya walkerana

Height 8 to 9 in. Flower 1 in.

DWARF COMPARETTIA ORCHID
Comparettia falcata

along the creeping stem of the plant are one or two sweet-smelling flowers. Blooming in winter and spring, the flowers last up to six weeks.

HOW TO GROW. The dwarf cattleya grows best in temperatures from 55° to 60° at night and from 65° to 75° in the daytime. It requires abundant diffused sunlight, or 14 to 16 hours of very bright artificial light daily. Keep humidity between 50 and 60 per cent. Pot the orchids in a mixture of 7 parts fir bark to 1 part redwood bark, 1 part perlite and 1 part coarse peat moss; or use a commercial potting mixture formulated for cattleyas. The plant can also be mounted on a slab of tree fern or cork bark.

Water sparingly between the blooming period and the start of new growth. When growth begins, water about once a week but allow the medium to become nearly dry between waterings. Fertilize potted plants at every third watering during active growth with a high-nitrogen formula such as 30-10-10; give slab-mounted plants a balanced formula such as 18-18-18. Dilute fertilizers to half the strength recommended on the label. When pseudobulbs stop growing larger, reduce water and withhold fertilizer for two weeks.

If a dwarf cattleya orchid outgrows its container or if the growing medium has begun to deteriorate and does not drain well, repot it as new roots are forming. Propagate additional plants by dividing the plant stem, leaving three or four pseudobulbs in each clump.

COMPARETTIA
Comp. falcata; Comp. macroplectron (dwarf comparettia orchid)

Graceful little orchids, these comparettias drape in arching sprays above clusters of dwarf pseudobulbs, each with a bright green leaf about 4 inches long. The flowers' stalks, 8 or 9 inches tall, carry three to eight blooms each. From fall to winter, *Comp. falcata* produces 1-inch hooded pink flowers with tiny spurs that are cerise or rose-violet. *Comp. macroplectron* has 2-inch flowers with spurs of the same length, blooming in summer and fall. The flowers are pink or violet with spots of rose or purple.

HOW TO GROW. Comparettia orchids grow best in intermediate temperatures of 55° to 60° at night and 65° to 75° during the daytime. Give them indirect or curtain-filtered sunlight or bright artificial light for 14 to 16 hours a day. Keep the humidity between 50 and 70 per cent. Plant them in small clay pots containing a mixture of 7 parts of fir bark to 1 part redwood bark, 1 part perlite and 1 part coarse peat moss; or in a greenhouse, attach them to slabs of tree fern or cork bark, adding small amounts of fresh sphagnum moss beneath the roots. Keep the growing medium constantly moist since the roots must never dry out. Comparettia orchids are never completely dormant, but less water is needed just before they bloom.

At every third watering, fertilize potted plants with a nitrogen-rich formula, such as 30-10-10, and slab-mounted plants with a balanced formula such as 18-18-18; dilute either to half the strength recommended on the label. Replace the top layer of potting mixture in early spring each year. Repot comparettias when they outgrow their pots or when the growing medium begins to deteriorate and does not drain well. Propagate new plants by division, keeping three or more pseudobulbs in each clump.

DENDROBIUM
D. jenkinsii (dwarf dendrobium orchid)

This dwarf orchid species adapts readily to miniature gardening, not only because of its size, 1 to 2 inches high, but because it grows best when crowded in a small pot. Each pseudobulb bears a single evergreen leaf and, in spring, a spike of two or three orange-yellow flowers each 1 inch wide. The fragrant blooms have downy, ruffled lips and last for two to three weeks.

HOW TO GROW. The dwarf dendrobium grows best when the temperature is 55° to 60° at night and 65° to 75° in the daytime; lower the night temperature to 50° to start flowering. Give the plant bright sunlight with only enough shading to prevent it from burning or drying out. If grown under artificial light it will need 14 to 16 hours of exposure per day, supplemented by as much sunlight as possible; the species does not thrive under artificial light alone. Maintain high humidity of 50 to 70 per cent.

Pot this dendrobium in a mixture of 7 parts fir bark to 1 part redwood bark, 1 part perlite and 1 part coarse peat moss. It may also be attached to a slab of tree fern or cork bark. Keep the plant moist at all times, reducing the amount of water as flowering begins. Good drainage is important. Fertilize potted plants twice a month with a high-nitrogen formula such as 30-10-10 and slab-mounted plants with a balanced formula such as 18-18-18; dilute fertilizer to half the strength recommended on the label. If plants have outgrown their pots or if the medium begins to deteriorate and does not drain well, repot dendrobiums as their new roots are forming. Propagate them by division, keeping three or four pseudobulbs in each clump.

MASDEVALLIA
Masd. chontalensis; Masd. lilliputiana; Masd. simula (miniature masdevallia orchid)

These orchids, which are among the smallest of the tree-dwelling masdevallias, offer an abundant display of delicate flowers whose sepals form a tubular hood that splits into tapering tail-like appendages. The ¾-inch-long flowers of *Masd. chontalensis* are white tipped with yellow, and they contrast richly with the dark green, shiny leaves. Although masdevallia orchids usually bloom in winter, they may appear throughout the year.

Masd. lilliputiana, the smallest of the genus, forms a dense thatch of leaves, each ¾ inch long, crowded by dozens of sharp-lipped flowers ¼ inch wide and ⅜ inch long. The flowers, cream colored with red spots, continue to appear for a good part of the summer. *Masd. simula* has bright green leaves 2 to 4 inches long and yellow flowers barred with coral or purple. Half an inch in diameter, the flowers have spatulate, rose-purple lips. They bloom from late spring to midsummer and sporadically throughout the year.

HOW TO GROW. Masdevallias grow best in a cool greenhouse with night temperatures of 50° to 55° and day temperatures of 60° to 70°. Give them bright artificial light for 14 to 16 hours a day, or indirect or curtain-filtered sunlight. Full sun may scorch the foliage. Maintain high humidity of 50 to 70 per cent.

Masdevallias grow best in small containers, either in slatted baskets containing osmunda or tree-fern chunks or in pots containing a mixture of 7 parts fir bark to 1 part redwood bark, 1 part perlite and 1 part peat moss. The potting medium should be evenly moist but never soggy. Fertilize basket plants every other month with a balanced formula such as 18-18-18, and potted plants with a high-nitrogen formula such as 30-10-10; dilute fertilizer to half the strength recommended on the label. Repot as new growth starts, either when the plant has outgrown its pot or if the growing medium has begun to deteriorate and does not drain well. Propagate by division of clumps.

For climate zones, see map, page 151.

Height 1 to 2 in. Flower 1 in.

DWARF DENDROBIUM ORCHID
Dendrobium jenkinsii

Height ¾ in. Flower ¼ in.

MINIATURE MASDEVALLIA ORCHID
Masdevallia lilliputiana

House plants, page 123;   Orchids, page 131;   Rock garden plants, page 134;   Roses, page 143;   Vegetables and fruits, page 145.

Height 2½ in. Flower 1 to 1¼ in.

SAMURAI ORCHID
Neofinetia falcata

Height 2 to 3 in. Flower 1 in.

DWARF SOPHRONITELLA ORCHID
Sophronitella violacea

NEOFINETIA

Neof. falcata, also called *Angraecum falcatum* (samurai orchid)

On stems only 2 to 2½ inches tall, the samurai orchid bears alternating pairs of light green fleshy leaves. Clusters of milk-white flowers 1 to 1¼ inches in diameter bloom in summer and autumn on 3- to 4-inch stalks. Each flower has slender, back-curving sepals and petals, and gives off a sweet fragrance, especially at night.

HOW TO GROW. Neofinetia grows best in 40 to 50 per cent humidity and temperatures of 55° to 60° at night and 65° to 75° in the daytime. Give it bright indirect or filtered sunlight or bright artificial light for 14 to 16 hours a day.

Plant the samurai orchid in a small pot containing a tightly packed mixture of 7 parts fir bark to 1 part redwood bark, 1 part perlite and 1 part coarse peat moss. After potting, water sparingly until the roots are established. When the plant is actively growing, keep the medium moist but not soggy. Fertilize with every third watering, using a high-nitrogen formula such as 30-10-10 diluted to half the strength recommended on the label. After flowering, reduce water and withhold fertilizer until leaf growth resumes. Train aerial roots into the pot by moistening and bending them into the growing mixture. Repot the samurai orchid when the medium has begun to deteriorate and does not drain well. Propagate additional plants by division of offshoots when these begin to develop new roots.

SAMURAI ORCHID See *Neofinetia*

SOPHRONITELLA

S. violacea (dwarf sophronitella orchid)

This midget orchid bears bright rose-to-violet flowers only 1 inch wide. Its narrow pseudobulbs, growing in a dense cluster, are ½ to 1¼ inches tall. The thin, dark, glossy evergreen leaves are 2 to 3 inches long. Blooms, two or three to a short stalk, open sequentially over two to three weeks in winter. The sepals and petals are narrow and oblong. The lip of the orchid is usually a darker shade of violet than is the rest of the flower.

HOW TO GROW. The sophronitella orchid grows best in intermediate temperatures of 55° to 60° at night and 65° to 75° during the day. It needs indirect sunlight or 14 to 16 hours a day of bright artificial light. Keep humidity at 40 to 60 per cent. Plant in a 2-inch pot containing a mixture of 7 parts fir bark to 1 part redwood bark, 1 part perlite and 1 part coarse peat moss; or mount it on a slab of tree fern or cork bark with a small patch of osmunda under the roots. The plant should be allowed to dry between waterings and needs good drainage.

During periods of active growth, fertilize dwarf sophronitella orchids once a week, giving a potted plant a high-nitrogen formula such as 30-10-10 and a slab-mounted plant a balanced formula such as 18-18-18; dilute either to half the strength recommended on the label. Withhold fertilizer when the plant is not actively growing. Repot when the growing medium begins to deteriorate and drains poorly. Propagate when new growth starts by dividing the plant into clumps of three or four pseudobulbs.

Rock-garden plants

ANACYCLUS

A. depressus (Atlas daisy)

Hairy, gray fernlike leaves cover the creeping, ground-hugging stems of the Atlas daisy as they form clumps that are about 2 inches high and 12 inches wide. In summer, the plant bears low daisy-like flowers with white petals that have red backs. This spreading perennial thrives in a trough or in rock gardens.

HOW TO GROW. Atlas daisy is hardy in Zones 6-10 but should be mulched in winter in the northern zones. Provide a location where it will receive full sun and a well-drained, gravelly soil with an alkaline pH of 7.0 to 8.0. Plant in spring or fall. Remove faded flowers to lengthen the flowering season. Propagate additional plants from seeds or by dividing clumps in the spring.

AQUILEGIA
A. flabellata 'Pumila' (fan columbine); *A. jonesii* (Jones columbine)

Hardy perennials that form small airy mounds of finely divided foliage, miniature columbines bear funnel-shaped flowers with long spurs in late spring and early summer. The fan columbine Pumila has blue-green leaves and grows up to 6 inches high with a spread of 12 inches. Its flowers, 1 to 1½ inches long, are carried on 12-inch stems in spring and early summer. This variety often has a life span longer than the columbine's usual three years. The Jones columbine is stemless and has round leaves that form tiny clumps. In early spring, a single ½-inch blue or purple flower rises above the foliage of each plant.

HOW TO GROW. Columbines grow throughout Zones 3-10 except in Florida and along the Gulf Coast. They do best in partial shade but they tolerate full sun except in hot, dry areas. Plant them in moist, gravelly soil with organic matter mixed into it to provide an acid pH of 5.0 to 6.0. Allow the soil to dry somewhat between waterings in summer. In the late fall, give columbines in Zones 3-5 a light organic mulch such as hay or straw. Fertilize the plants in spring and fall with dried manure. Propagate additional plants from seed in spring or fall.

ATLAS DAISY See *Anacyclus*

BABIES'-BREATH See *Gypsophila*

CAMPANULA
C. allionii; C. cochleariifolia 'Alba'; *C. elatines garganica* (Adriatic bellflower); *C. lilacina; C. pulla; C. raineri; C. stansfeldii; C. haylodgensis* 'Warley White' (Warley white bellflower) (all called bellflower)

Most of the smaller varieties of this large and diverse genus are creeping perennials that form dense mats. The serrated leaves are often in the shapes of fans or shells, and the flaring, bell-shaped flowers appear from early to late summer. Bellflowers are excellent planted in rock or alpine gardens, containers, wall plantings or between flagstones. The elongated, hairy leaves of *C. allionii* are 2 inches long and form rosettes. In early summer, each 2- to 5-inch flower stalk bears a single erect or nodding flower that is 1¾ inches long and may be lavender or white. The 4- to 6-inch-high spreading mats of shell-shaped leaves of *C. cochleariifolia* 'Alba' are useful as ground cover. White flowers ½ inch long appear from July to September on 3-inch stems. Adriatic bellflower has small, crinkled leaves that are covered with shiny hairs and 5- to 6-inch erect or trailing flower stems that bear blue-purple flowers with white centers. The flowers are less than ½ inch long and bloom continuously throughout the summer months.

C. pulla has glossy, 1-inch leaves that grow in rosettes 3 to 4 inches high. In June, solitary deep-purple flowers nod at

Height 2 in. Flower 2 in. Spread 12 in.

ATLAS DAISY
Anacyclus depressus

Height 6 in. Flower 1 to 1½ in. Spread 12 in.

FAN COLUMBINE
Aquilegia flabellata pumila

For climate zones, see map, page 151.

House plants, page 123;   Orchids, page 131;   Rock garden plants, page 134;   Roses, page 143;   Vegetables and fruits, page 145.

the ends of 2- to 6-inch flower stems. The gray oval leaves of *C. raineri* form tufts that are 3 to 4 inches high, above which bloom upward-facing blue flowers 1¼ inches long. The hybrid *C. stansfeldii* is a variety that is especially easy to grow. Its pale green, slightly hairy leaves are 2 inches long and form broad mats 5 inches high. From June to August, the plant is covered with branched sprays of drooping, dark purple flowers. Warley white bellflower has sharply toothed oval leaves on slender stems that also bear single or double white flowers ½ inch long.

HOW TO GROW. Adriatic bellflower and *C. stansfeldii* are hardy from Zone 5 south, while *C. cochleariifolia* 'Alba' and *C. pulla* will grow from Zone 6 south. The other bellflowers may be grown in Zones 4-10. Shade is necessary in areas where the summers are hot; otherwise, grow in full sun or partial shade. Provide a moist but well-drained sandy loam with a pH of 6.0 to 7.0, and fertilize the plants each spring with dried manure. Propagate from seed sown in early fall, from cuttings taken during the active growing season, or by division in early spring.

COLUMBINE See *Aquilega*
CRANE'S-BILL GERANIUM See *Geranium*

DIANTHUS

D. alpinus (alpine pink); *D. deltoides* 'Nanus,' also called *D. glauca nana* (dwarf maiden pink); *D. freynii; D. microlepis; D. microlepis* 'Musalae,' also called *D. musaliae; D. myrtinervius,* also called *D. peristeria; D. roysii; D. subacaulis* (all called pinks)

Pinks are hardy evergreen perennials that are invaluable when planted among paving stones or in a rock garden, rock wall or container. The narrow grasslike leaves are often blue- or gray-green and form dense, spreading mats. The long-lasting flowers are sometimes fragrant and usually appear over a long blooming season. Most varieties have a flattened flower with five petals that are often fringed. Pink and red are the most common colors, and flowers may also be bicolored or spotted.

The alpine pink's smooth, dark green foliage spreads slowly to form an inch-high mat. Blooming profusely in late spring on stems 3 to 5 inches long, the 1½-inch flowers are rose-pink speckled with white. The dwarf maiden pink sows itself easily, is a fast grower and has trailing stems, making it ideal as a ground cover or trailing over rocks or walls. The dark green, glaucous leaves form a mat 2 inches tall, and the deep pink to red flowers are ¾ inch wide and appear in late spring and early summer. *D. freynii* has blue-gray leaves and grows 2 to 4 inches tall. Its brilliant pink, ¾-inch flowers have sharply toothed edges.

The clumps of *D. microlepis* are composed of ¾- to 1-inch-long leaves; in early to midsummer ½-inch wide red-purple flowers appear on stems that are 2 to 4 inches long. *D. microlepis* 'Musalae' is similar, but its stems are longer and more slender. The bearded pink ½-inch-wide flowers of *D. myrtinervius* are borne from late spring to midsummer, rising above mats of glaucous leaves that are 1 to 2 inches tall. A hybrid, *D. roysii* grows 3 inches tall and produces vivid pink flowers throughout the summer months, while *D. subacaulis* grows 1-inch-high tufts of gray leaves less than ½ inch long and bears pale to bright pink flowers that are ⅝ inch across.

HOW TO GROW. The alpine pink and dwarf maiden pink are hardy, with protection, up to Zone 2. In areas with little snow cover they will need a light mulch during the winter months. Other pinks are hardy in Zones 4-7. Cool, moist summers are best; where summers are hot, provide some

Height 5 to 6 in. Flower ½ in.

ADRIATIC BELLFLOWER
Campanula elatines garganica

Height 4 in. Flower 1 to 1½ in.

ALPINE PINK
Dianthus alpinus

Bulbs, page 98;   Cacti and succulents, page 105;   Evergreens, page 110;   Ferns, page 119;   Grasses, shrubs and trees, page 121;

shade. Grow pinks in well-drained, light sandy soil. Although these plants prefer a neutral soil, they will tolerate slightly acid conditions.

Although pinks are easily started from seed, seedlings are not always true to type. To maintain a specific variety, propagate additional plants by division, cuttings or layering. Pinks grow and bloom best when they are two or three years old and should be divided when they appear to be crowded or when blooms diminish.

DRABA

D. aizoides (whitlow grass); *D. bruniifolia olympica* (Olympic draba); *D. dedeana; D. mollissima; D. siberica* (Siberian draba)

Particularly adaptable to alpine and rock gardens, low-growing evergreen draba is found in the loose, rocky soil of mountainous areas throughout the world. A deep taproot helps this woolly perennial survive its harsh environment. The narrow, hairy leaves grow in mounds of closely packed rosettes and are usually gray-green.

Whitlow grass grows in dense tufts 4 inches tall, with a spread of 6 to 9 inches. Above the ½-inch-long leaves rise spikes that bear many yellow flowers. Olympic draba forms clumps 2 to 4 inches tall of ¼-inch dark green leaves and bears orange flowers on downy spikes that rise slightly above the foliage. The flowers of *D. dedeana* are usually white, but are occasionally pale yellow. Leaves ¼ inch long form a dense mat 2 inches tall. *D. mollissima* reaches only 1 inch in height, but may spread 6 inches or more. In May and June it bears bright yellow cross-shaped flowers that are from ⅓ to ½ inch wide, producing as many as 18 blooms on each spike. The slender, creeping stems of Siberian draba may grow 12 inches in length, forming loose, open rosettes 2 to 6 inches high. This species, which bears yellow flowers in both spring and fall, grows faster and is easier to cultivate than Whitlow grass or Olympic draba.

HOW TO GROW. Whitlow grass thrives in Zone 4 and can be grown in the northern parts of Zone 5, while Olympic draba is hardy through Zone 6. Siberian draba is the hardiest species and can be grown in Zones 3-5. All need full sun, with partial shade during the summer. Drabas do best in well-drained, gravelly soil with organic matter such as leaf mold incorporated. Keep them moist during the growing and flowering season, but water sparingly the rest of the year, being careful not to get water on the foliage. Propagate additional plants from seeds in March or April, or from cuttings of nonflowering rosettes in June or July. Drabas are generally free of pests and diseases.

EDRAIANTHUS

E. pumilio; E. serpyllifolius; E. tenuifolius (all called grassy bells)

Grassy bells are flowering perennials that tolerate cold winters. They form low-growing mats. Narrow leaves cover stems that creep along the ground; flaring flowers appear singly or in clusters at the ends of the stems. *E. pumilio* grows in a clump 2 to 3 inches tall, with slightly hairy leaves 1 inch long and deep purple 1-inch flowers. *E. serpyllifolius* forms a 1-inch-high mat, with violet or white flowers up to 2 inches across appearing around its edges. *E. tenuifolius* also has creeping stems and forms a mat 3 to 6 inches tall. Violet-blue flowers 1 inch across appear in clusters of a dozen or so in late spring and early summer.

HOW TO GROW. Grassy bells grow in Zones 5-10, except in Florida and along the Gulf Coast. They tolerate full sun or partial shade and they require a well-drained gravelly soil

Height 2 in. Flower ½ in.

Draba mollissima

Height 2 to 3 in. Flower 1 in.

GRASSY BELLS
Edraianthus pumilio

For climate zones, see map, page 151.

House plants, page 123;   Orchids, page 131;   Rock garden plants, page 134;   Roses, page 143;   Vegetables and fruits, page 145.

STEMLESS GENTIAN
Gentiana acaulis

CRANE'S-BILL
Geranium sanguineum prostratum

with a pH of 7.0 to 8.0. Allow the soil to dry slightly between waterings; water well in times of drought. Fertilize the plants with dried manure in spring and fall. Propagate grassy bells from seeds or divisions in the spring.

FLAX See *Linum*

GENTIAN See *Gentiana*

GENTIANA

G. acaulis (stemless gentian); *G. angustifolia; G. clusii; G. lagodechiana; G. saxosa; G. verna,* also called *G. angulosa* (spring gentian)

The intense blue color of trumpet-shaped gentian flowers makes these eye-catching plants to grow in rock and alpine gardens. Natives of mountainous regions, gentians usually form dense clumps and produce their attractive flowers in spring or summer.

The evergreen leaves of stemless gentian are 1 inch long and form rosettes that are 4 inches tall, above which rise rich blue green-throated flowers that are 2 to 3 inches long. *G. angustifolia* is similar to stemless gentian but its leaves are slightly more elongated, while *G. clusii* is distinguished by its leathery leaves and the olive-green throat of its summer-blooming blue flowers. The creeping, slender stems of *G. lagodechiana* may grow to 15 inches in length and bear 1-inch leaves. During late summer and early autumn, green-spotted blue flowers are produced along the stems and at the tips. *G. saxosa,* a New Zealand species, has succulent, dark green to bronze-green leaves that form loose, open rosettes. In late summer and early fall, each sprawling, 6-inch-long flower stem bears a single white-and-brown-striped bloom. Spring gentian is one of the smallest members of the family, with oval leaves and blue flowers no more than an inch long.

HOW TO GROW. Stemless gentian grows in Zones 3 and 4, spring gentian in Zones 6-8. *G. clusii, G. angustifolia, G. lagodechiana* and *G. saxosa* are hardy in Zones 5-7. For best growth, these alpines need cool, moist summers. Given these conditions, they will thrive in full sun; where the soil is warmer and drier, they need partial shade. Provide a rich, slightly gravelly, well-drained loam. Fertilize plants in spring with dried manure or ordinary fertilizer. Gentians are easily grown from fresh seed, but they may also be started from cuttings or divisions.

GERANIUM

G. sanguineum prostratum, also called *G. lancastriense* (crane's-bill)

Deeply cut leaves give a feathery texture to crane's-bill, a perennial that will bloom from early summer to early fall. It grows 4 to 6 inches tall with a spread of 18 inches; its trailing stems form a thick mat. The flowers are pink with red veins. In the autumn, the leaves turn bright red. The plant is useful as a low ground cover or an edging plant, or it can be grown in a dry stone wall.

HOW TO GROW. Dwarf crane's-bill is hardy in Zones 4-10, thriving in full sun but tolerating partial shade. Plants grow well in almost any garden soil with a pH of 6.5 to 8.0. Propagate additional plants from stem cuttings taken in the summer or from seeds sown in either spring or fall; clumps should not be divided.

GRASSY BELLS See *Edraianthus*

GYPSOPHILA

G. cerastioides (mouse-ear gypsophila); *G. muralis* (cushion

Height 4 in. Flower 2 to 3 in.

Height 4 to 6 in. Flower 1 in. Spread 18 in.

gypsophila); *G. repens* 'Fratensis' (creeping gypsophila) (all called babies'-breath)

Whether tumbling over small garden rocks or tucked into a crevice of a stone wall, the low-growing species of babies'-breath create a delicate summer mist of tiny blooms. Mouse-ear gypsophila, named for its downy gray leaves, is 2 to 3 inches tall and spreads 12 to 18 inches. A tender perennial, it bears white, red-veined flowers ⅛ to ½ inch wide from late spring until frost. Cushion gypsophila is an annual that grows 6 to 8 inches tall and spreads up to 2 feet. Its bell-shaped pink flowers appear from midsummer to frost. Creeping gypsophila usually grows 3 to 6 inches tall and spreads 1½ to 2 feet. This alpine perennial is the hardiest of the three. Its ⅓-inch white to deep pink flowers bloom in summer surrounded by gray-green leaves.

HOW TO GROW. Mouse-ear gypsophila is winter hardy only in Zones 7 and 8 and in Zone 9 on the West Coast; cushion gypsophila will grow from seed each year in Zones 4-8; and creeping gypsophila flourishes in Zones 3-8. All three species grow well if they are given full sun and well-drained neutral or slightly alkaline soil.

Plant the two perennials in early spring, spacing them 12 to 15 inches apart. In Zones 4 and 5, cover plants in the late fall with a mulch of hay or straw. Because the perennials do not spread underground, mounds can be left undisturbed indefinitely. Sow cushion gypsophila seeds in spring when the danger of frost is past; sowing at two- to four-week intervals will give you continuous summer flowers. Thin seedlings to stand 8 to 12 inches apart.

Propagate mouse-ear gypsophila by dividing plants in the early spring or fall. Creeping gypsophila can be propagated from 2-inch cuttings taken in spring.

HAREBELL See *Campanula*

LINUM

L. elegans 'Gemmell's Hybrid'; *L. flavum* 'Compactum' (dwarf flowering flax)

Graceful, delicate dwarf flowering flax blooms throughout the summer months, bearing yellow, five-petaled flowers up to 1 inch across. Gemmell's Hybrid, a dwarf 6 to 9 inches tall, has creeping stems with small, narrow leaves. On the more erect Compactum, leaves are broader and dark green; clumps grow up to 6 inches tall.

HOW TO GROW. Dwarf flowering flax grows in Zones 5-10 except in Florida and along the Gulf Coast. It needs full sun and well-drained soil. To keep plants blooming over a long period, remove faded flowers. Fertilize with dried manure or a balanced fertilizer such as 10-10-10 in spring and fall. In the fall, cover the plants in Zone 5 with a light organic mulch such as hay or straw. Start new plants with cuttings taken from nonflowering stems in summer, or sow seeds in spring. Flax plants should not be divided.

LOBULARIA

L. maritima 'Violet Queen' (dwarf sweet alyssum)

Spreading mounds of this fragrant flower bloom from late spring to the first frost. Only 4 inches tall, they are frequently used to edge outdoor planters and can be tucked into a rock garden. The ¼-inch violet flowers have a fragrance similar to that of honeysuckle; the flower clusters are surrounded by small, downy leaves that are ½ to 1½ inches long. Sweet alyssum is a tender perennial, usually treated as an annual in the North.

HOW TO GROW. Dwarf sweet alyssum is evergreen year round in Zones 9 and 10, but from Zone 8 northward to Zone

For climate zones, see map, page 151.

Height 3 to 6 in. Flower ⅓ in. Spread 1½ to 2 ft.

CREEPING BABIES' BREATH
Gypsophila repens 'Fratensis'

Height 6 to 9 in. Flower 1 in.

DWARF FLOWERING FLAX
Linum elegans 'Gemmell's Hybrid'

House plants, page 123;   Orchids, page 131;   Rock garden plants, page 134;   Roses, page 143;   Vegetables and fruits, page 145.

DWARF SWEET ALYSSUM
Lobularia maritima 'Violet Queen'

Height 4 in. Flower ¼ in.

SILVER-EDGED PRIMROSE
Primula marginata

Height 4 in. Flower 1 in. Spread 5 in.

4 it must be planted annually. It flourishes in full sun in almost any well-drained garden soil. Sow seeds in the early spring as soon as the ground can be worked or start seedlings indoors four to six weeks before the last spring frost is due. Transplant seedlings to the garden once the danger of frost is past, setting them about 6 inches apart. An additional sowing in early summer may produce a generous crop of fall flowers. If plants are cut back severely, they will sometimes bloom more profusely later in the same season.

Alyssum often seeds itself. Additional plants may also be propagated by taking stem cuttings 2 to 3 inches long, rooting them during the summer and keeping them in a cold frame until the following spring.

MARIGOLD See *Tagetes*

PANSY See *Viola*
PINKS See *Dianthus*
PRIMROSE See *Primula*

PRIMULA
P. frondosa (Balkan primrose); *P. juliae* 'Wanda' (Wanda primrose); *P. marginata* (silver-edged primrose)

These ground-hugging perennials with brilliant flowers are used in low borders or to brighten rock gardens. The Balkan primrose grows up to 5 inches tall; in spring it bears clusters of rose-pink flowers each ½ inch wide. Leaves that are dark green above and silvery beneath form 6-inch rosettes. The hybrid Wanda bears wine-red flowers 1 inch wide on 2-inch stems from early to midspring. They grow from low clumps of wrinkled foliage. These clumps multiply to form an evergreen mat. Silver-edged primrose, with toothed leaf margins marked with white, grows in 5-inch clumps that are striking when massed. In spring it produces clusters of lavender primroses, each 1 inch wide.

HOW TO GROW. Balkan primrose is hardy in Zones 6-8, Wanda in Zones 4-8 and silver-edged primrose in Zones 5-8. They all grow best in areas with cool, moist summers, but Wanda withstands warm, dry conditions better than the others. Plant in partial shade in an acid soil (pH 5.0 to 6.0) supplemented with such organic matter as peat moss or leaf mold. Keep the soil constantly moist. In late fall give the plants a light mulch such as hay or straw. Fertilize these primroses with dry manure or a balanced fertilizer such as 10-10-10 in spring and fall.

Propagate additional plants from seed or by dividing the clumps immediately after flowering. Division is necessary every two or three years.

SAXIFRAGA
S. allioni, also called *S. moshata; S. arco valleyi; S. boydii, S. cochlearis minor* (snail saxifrage); *S. grisebachii* 'Wisley'; *S. kabschia* 'Cranbourne'; *S. kabschia* 'Ferdinandi-Coburgi'; *S. retusa* (all called saxifrage)

These small, cold-resistant perennials grow in mosslike mounds or dense tufts. Their tiny flowers rise above the leaves on thin, wiry stalks in the spring or summer. Most are alpine plants, suitable for use in pockets of stone walls or in rock gardens. The varieties listed here fall into four of the 16 groups of saxifrages.

The most popular, with many modern hybrids, are the kabschia saxifrages that spread with creeping stems to form low cushions and bear flat flowers in very early spring. *S. arco valleyi,* with silver-gray leaves, has pink flowers on stalks 1 inch tall. *S. boydii* forms a dense tuft of blue-gray leaves and has 2-inch flower stems each carrying two yellow blooms. Two kabschia hybrids grow only 1 inch tall but spread 9 to 12 inches wide; Cranbourne grows in a gray-green tuft with ¾-inch pink flowers; Ferdinandi-Coburgi produces silver-green rosettes and yellow flowers about ½ inch across. *S. grisebachii* carries tiny red blooms ⅙ inch wide above a silver-green mat 6 to 9 inches tall and 9 to 12 inches wide. The latter is sometimes called Engleria.

Dactyloide saxifrages grow in mossy blankets; hardy *S. allioni* produces bright green cushions up to 3 inches tall and 18 inches wide, with ½-inch flat yellow or white flowers in the early spring. Euaizoonia saxifrages have broad leaves that are often silver-tinged because they are encrusted with lime; *S. cochlearis minor* grows in a mound up to 4 inches tall and 1 foot wide, bearing ½-inch white flowers in the early summer. Porphyrion saxifrages form low creeping mats; *S. retusa* makes a dark green tuft that is 1 inch tall and 12 inches wide from which ⅓-inch purple flowers bloom in scant clusters in the spring.

HOW TO GROW. All of these saxifrages are winter hardy in Zones 4-6. They grow best in well-drained gritty or rocky alkaline soil with a pH of 7.0 to 7.5. Although they tolerate full sun in northern zones, they generally do best with partial shade. Set out plants in the early spring as soon as the danger of frost is past or in early fall. If brown patches develop on old plants, revive them with a fine top dressing of sifted loam, leaf mold and sand.

Propagate additional plants by dividing after flowering or by cutting off nonflowering little plants that, in some species, develop around the parent plant.

SAXIFRAGE See *Saxifraga*
SWEET ALYSSUM See *Lobularia*

TAGETES

T. patula nana (dwarf French marigold); *T. signata pumila*, also called *T. tenuifolia pumila* (dwarf marigold, signet marigold)

Less than a third the size of standard marigolds, these summer-blooming annuals flourish in almost every region of the United States. Their pungently scented flowers range from deep yellow and orange to brownish red and dark mahogany. Dwarf French marigolds grow 6 to 8 inches tall and spread about a foot, bearing solitary flowers 1 to 2 inches wide. The variety Dainty Marietta has single yellow flowers with mahogany centers while Helen Chapman bears double golden flowers with red centers. The double flowers of Pigmy Primrose are dark yellow with red centers.

Dwarf marigolds range from 6 to 10 inches tall with fine, fernlike leaves and yellow or golden orange flowers 1 inch wide. Two good varieties are Gnome, which bears single orange flowers on 6-inch stems, and Little Lulu, which has bright yellow blooms on 7-inch stems.

HOW TO GROW. Dwarf marigolds can be grown in all zones. They thrive in full sun in any garden soil and will tolerate poor, dry conditions, but they should be watered during periods of extended drought. Buy young plants from a nursery and set them in the garden when frost is no longer a threat. You may also sow seeds outdoors at this time, or start seeds indoors four to six weeks before the last spring frost is expected. Set seeds or young seedlings in the garden about 6 inches apart. In Zones 9 and 10 marigold seed can be sown outdoors at any time.

Pinching off dead flowers encourages branching and more blooms. When cutting flowers for bouquets, remove the bottom leaves so that the water will not become murky. Marigolds are usually untroubled by pests.

For climate zones, see map, page 151.

Height 1 in. Flower ½ in. Spread 9 to 12 in.

SAXIFRAGE
Saxifraga kabschia 'Ferdinandi-Coburgi'

Height 6 to 8 in. Flower 1 in. Spread 12 in.

DWARF FRENCH MARIGOLD
Tagetes patula nana 'Dainty Marietta'

House plants, page 123;   Orchids, page 131;   Rock garden plants, page 134;   Roses, page 143;   Vegetables and fruits, page 145.

WOOLLY THYME
Thymus pseudolanuginosus

Leaves 1/16 to 1/8 in. long

WILD PANSY
Viola tricolor 'Heartsease'

Height 4 to 6 in. Flower 1 in.

THYME See *Thymus*

THYMUS

T. citriodorus 'Aureus' (variegated lemon-scented thyme); *T. doerfleri minus; T. herba-barona* (caraway thyme); *T. praecox* 'Coccineus,' also known as *T. serpyllum* 'Coccineus' (red mother-of-thyme); *T. pseudolanuginosus* (woolly thyme)

Best known as a culinary herb, perennial thyme is also a useful ornament in the landscape. With trailing stems that form a dense carpet several inches thick, thyme is attractive planted in dry walls, in rock crevices, on slopes, between flagstones, in rock gardens and as a ground cover. Most types of thyme have oval, evergreen leaves ¼ to ½ inch long on thin, woody stems, and bloom during the summer. The flowers attract bees.

Variegated lemon-scented thyme is a hybrid with smooth, aromatic leaves that are marked with yellow. It grows only 6 inches high and bears pale lilac flowers. *T. doerfleri minus* carries reddish-purple flowers above white stems and leaves that are densely covered with long and short hairs. Caraway thyme is best used between flagstones where its dark green leaves and clusters of purple flowers release their scent when they are walked upon. From a species that has many variations comes red mother-of-thyme, with its dark, red-green leaves and its bright red-purple flowers. Woolly thyme has leaves and stems that are covered with gray-white down; its flowers are pink.

HOW TO GROW. Variegated lemon-scented thyme, caraway thyme and *T. doerfleri minus* will grow in Zones 4-10; red mother-of-thyme and woolly thyme are hardy in Zone 3 as well. All require full sun, and do best in light, well-drained soil with a pH of 5.5 to 7.0. Fertilize plants only once a year, in early spring, by scratching a tablespoon of bone meal or cottonseed meal into the soil around each plant; do not feed the plants again since additional fertilizer would encourage late growth, making them susceptible to winter injury. Where the temperatures in winter are likely to stay below zero for long periods, protect the plants with a mulch of salt hay or straw in late fall. Spring pruning to encourage new growth will keep mature plants from becoming woody and losing their fragrance. When plants become overgrown after several years, they should be divided.

VIOLA

V. alpina; V. arenaria rosea, also called *V. rupestris; V. biflora; V. hederacea* (Australian violet); *V. pinnata; V. tricolor* 'Heartsease' (wild pansy) (all called pansy)

These members of the pansy family, ranging from 1½ to 6 inches tall, are prized for the colorful variety of their delicate flowers. Composed of five overlapping petals, the flowers are ½ to 2 inches wide and resemble violets. Although these species are perennials, most gardeners grow them as annuals.

V. alpina, 1½ to 4 inches tall, bears 1-inch violet or deep purple flowers with white centers in early summer. *V. arenaria rosea* is 1 to 2 inches tall and bears tiny pale pink flowers from spring through summer. Each plant of *V. biflora* bears two dark-veined, bright yellow flowers in the spring, on stems 2½ to 6 inches tall. Australian violet grows 1½ to 3 inches tall along trailing stems; its summer-blooming purple flowers have white centers. *V. pinnata* is 2 to 3 inches tall; its scented blue-violet flowers are ½ inch long and appear in summer. Wild pansy, another summer flower, is variable in color; its flowers may be up to 1 inch wide on stems that are from 4 to 6 inches tall.

HOW TO GROW. Except for *V. arenaria rosea,* which is winter hardy as far north as Zone 3, these pansies must be planted anew each year in frost zones. In frost-free areas, they need to be replaced when flowering has diminished. These species grow best in partial shade, but they will tolerate sun if the summer temperature does not exceed 90°. Pansies need moist, well-drained soil that has been enriched with compost or leaf mold.

Sow seeds indoors 10 to 12 weeks before the last spring frost is expected. When frost danger has passed, plant seedlings or nursery plants in beds 4 to 6 inches apart. Seeds may be sown outdoors in summer to bloom the following spring if the seedlings are kept in a cold frame over winter. Cuttings taken in early summer or clumps divided in the fall may be rooted and kept in a cold frame until the following spring.

VIOLET See *Viola*

Roses
ROSA

R. hybrids (miniature roses)

The exquisite miniature roses, with perfectly proportioned small leaves, thorns, buds and flowers, are tiny counterparts of the large summer-blooming shrubs. They are ideal plants for rock gardens, rose-garden borders or indoor containers. Charming little flowers only ½ to 2 inches wide bloom almost continuously throughout the year indoors, and from spring to frost in the garden. With more than 300 varieties available, there are miniatures of many types of roses from hybrid teas and moss roses to cascading climbers. In a wide array of colors, they bloom on thin stems from 4 to 18 inches tall, lined with jagged-edged leaflets.

Si is the smallest rose of all. It usually grows only 4 to 6 inches tall indoors although it may reach 6 to 8 inches outdoors. Its ¼-inch buds open into pale pink semidouble flowers ¼ to ½ inch wide.

Medium-sized miniatures range in height from 6 to 10 inches. Kara grows very slowly, becoming only 6 to 8 inches tall. It is a miniature moss rose about one fifth the size of the garden standard. Like its large counterpart, it has buds and stems that are covered with soft green hairs. Its 1¼-inch five-petaled blooms open a deep pink and fade to muted rose. The oil that is secreted by the mossy hairs gives these plants a unique fragrance.

R. rouletii grows 6 to 12 inches tall; long blooming seasons begin when the plant is only 3 or 4 inches tall. Its slightly fragrant, pale pink double flowers are less than ½ inch wide. A popular house plant, *R. rouletii* is the parent of many modern miniatures. Varieties are available in white, pink, red and yellow as well as in blends.

Among somewhat larger species, miniature hybrid teas have tall, slowly opening buds that form spectacular flowers. These hardy miniatures grow 12 to 15 inches tall indoors and 18 inches or more in the garden. The following varieties have long-lasting blooms that are often exhibited in flower shows: Lavender Lace is a low, spreading shrub that produces fragrant, lavender-pink double flowers that are 1½ inches wide. Rise 'N' Shine bears golden-yellow flowers 1½ to 2 inches wide on a compact plant with proportionately large leaves. Starina, winner of many awards, has fragrant orange-to-red flowers 1½ inches wide.

There are also miniatures that mimic the familiar old-fashioned shrub roses. Simplex has arching stems that grow as much as 2 feet in the garden but usually remain under 18 inches indoors. It bears clusters of five-petaled flowers 1¼ inches wide. The apricot-colored buds open creamy white with yellow anthers at the center that become dark brown

Height 6 to 8 in. Flower 1¼ in.

MINIATURE ROSE
Rosa hybrid 'Kara'

Height 12 to 15 in. Flower 1½ in.

MINIATURE ROSE
Rosa hybrid 'Lavender Lace'

Height 4 to 6 in. Flower 1 in. Spread to 3 ft.

MINIATURE ROSE
Rosa hybrid 'Red Cascade'

For climate zones, see map, page 151.

Height 15 to 20 in. Flower 1½ in.

MINIATURE ROSE
Rosa hybrid 'Rise 'n' Shine'

Height 15 to 18 in. Flower 1¼ in.

MINIATURE ROSE
Rosa hybrid 'Simplex'

Height 12 to 16 in. Flower 1½ in.

MINIATURE ROSE
Rosa hybrid 'Starina'

after four or five days. Flowers grown indoors, as well as cut blooms, close at night but reopen in the morning. White Gem forms an upright shrub 12 to 18 inches tall with shiny, dark green leaves. Its fragrant, long-lasting white flowers are ¾ inch wide. Little Curt has very thorny stems that grow as tall as 3 feet in the garden but usually remains under 18 inches indoors. Its 1½-inch double flowers open flat to reveal showy stamens. The nearly black buds open into deep red flowers, good for cutting.

A climbing miniature rose is Red Cascade; its spreading, branching stems can be tied to a trellis, draped over a low stone wall or allowed to tumble from a hanging basket. The dark red double flowers are 1 inch wide; they bloom in clusters on arching side shoots 4 to 6 inches long.

HOW TO GROW. If raised indoors, miniature roses grow best in direct sunlight, or under very bright artificial light 14 to 16 hours a day. For abundant flowers, keep day temperatures between 70° and 75° and night temperatures between 60° and 65°. Maintain a relative humidity of 50 to 60 per cent by placing pots on a tray of moist gravel and by misting the plants lightly several times a day; allow the leaves to dry before evening.

Plant in 3-inch pots, using a mixture of 2 parts coarse sphagnum moss, 1 part coarse perlite and 1 part vermiculite. Firm the soil around the roots. Move a plant to a container one size larger before the roots become crowded. Keep the soil evenly moist to the touch but never soggy. Never let the roots get dry. During the growing season, fertilize miniature roses weekly, alternating a liquid fertilizer made for potted roses and a low-nitrogen house-plant fertilizer such as 5-8-7. Apply either fertilizer at one fourth the strength recommended on the label.

After they flower, let plants rest by placing them in filtered sunlight. Reduce the water for 6 to 8 weeks and do not fertilize. Following this rest period, prune off the previous year's growth to stimulate branching and flower production. Move the plants back into direct sunlight, resuming regular watering and fertilizing. Plants can be moved outdoors in summer and returned to the house in the fall. To prevent red spider mites, use clear water to wash the leaves at least once a week, especially the undersides. Propagate new roses from stem cuttings taken from new growth. If placed in moist vermiculite and heated from the bottom to 70°, cuttings should root in about four weeks.

Outdoors, miniature roses are hardy in Zones 6-10. They grow well where they receive at least four hours of direct sunlight a day. If humidity is low or the temperature very high, miniature roses need shade at noon.

Miniature roses grow best in slightly acid soil. They are usually sold in small pots but sometimes come with bare roots. Select healthy potted plants and set them outdoors in their containers in spring, allowing them to adjust to the climate before putting them into the ground. Place plants in prepared holes or beds where the garden soil has been mixed with equal parts of perlite and coarse sphagnum moss. In a damp climate, add vermiculite to assure proper drainage. Scatter 1 to 2 inches of a mulch such as salt hay, pine needles, bark chips or cocoa-bean hulls around each plant.

During the growing season, water thoroughly, soaking the soil to a depth of 10 to 12 inches. When plants receive 1 inch or more of rainfall a week there is no need to water. Fertilize plants during the growing season. You can apply a slow-release fertilizer in the early spring before growth starts, or sprinkle 5-10-5 fertilizer around the plant in early spring and when flowering begins.

To prevent insect damage and fungus disease, spray plants

with an all-purpose rose spray in the early spring just before growth starts and every eight to ten days during the growing season. In areas where winters are severe, protect plants from the cold by mounding loose soil over them in the fall or by covering the plant with a large can with both ends cut off, filling it with wood chips or straw. Remove such protection in early spring before growth starts.

Vegetables and fruits

ALPINE STRAWBERRY See *Fragaria*

BRASSICA

B. oleracea capitata hybrids (miniature cabbage)

Brightly colored, nutritious miniature cabbage is a vegetable attractive enough to grow as a border plant until it is ready to harvest. There are early- and late-maturing varieties less than half the size of standard cabbages. Pee Wee, Dwarf Morden, Little Leaguer and Junior are four early-season varieties with smooth green leaves. Pee Wee weighs only ½ pound when it matures in about 55 days. Dwarf Morden and Little Leaguer at 1 pound and Junior at 1½ pounds mature in 55 to 60 days. Two late-season 1- to 2-pound cabbages are Baby Head, which takes 70 days to mature, and Miniature Japanese Ornamental, a colorful cabbage with red-tinged leaves that matures in 65 days.

HOW TO GROW. Cabbages grow best with cool temperatures in average soils that are moist but well drained. Start early varieties indoors or in a hotbed six to eight weeks before the last spring frost is due, then set the seedlings in the garden two to three weeks before that last frost. Space them 6 to 8 inches apart in rows 12 to 15 inches apart. Late cabbage varieties can be sown directly in the garden in late summer. Space them the same distance as early varieties, grouping several seeds in each spot and thinning the groups to one plant when the seedlings are an inch tall. Fertilize the young cabbages at three- to four-week intervals, dusting about a cup of cottonseed meal on the soil for every 6 to 8 feet of row. Mulch around the plants to keep the soil moist and to minimize cultivation around the shallow roots. To control diseases, avoid planting cabbages where other cabbages or cabbage relatives such as broccoli or kale have grown within the four previous years.

CABBAGE See *Brassica*
CANTALOUPE See *Cucumis*
CARROT See *Daucus*

CITRULLUS

C. lanatus hybrids (miniature watermelon)

Tiny watermelons have the sweet, juicy taste of heavyweight melons, but they take up less space in both the garden and the refrigerator. New Hampshire Midget has a thin green rind and solid, deep red flesh; it matures in 70 days. Sugar Baby, which is light green with darker green stripes on its rind, has few seeds; it matures in 75 days. Golden Midget turns yellow when it is ripe, in about 65 days. These three midget varieties bear fruits 6 to 8 inches in diameter that weigh four to seven pounds. Their vines creep along the ground about 4 feet.

HOW TO GROW. Watermelons grow best in light, sandy, slightly acid soil with a pH of 6.0 to 7.0. Because these midget varieties mature faster than full-sized melons, they can be planted where the growing season is short. Melons require night temperatures above 55° and day temperatures of 80° or more. Where temperatures are cooler than this for

Diameter 4 in. Weight 1 lb.

MINIATURE CABBAGE
Brassica oleracea capitata 'Dwarf Morden'

Diameter 6 in. Weight 4 to 6 lbs.

MINIATURE WATERMELON
Citrullus lanatus 'New Hampshire Midget'

For climate zones, see map, page 151.

Diameter 4 in. Vine length 3 to 4 ft.

DWARF CANTALOUPE
Cucumis melo 'Minnesota Midget'

Length 3 to 4 in. Vine length 2 ft.

DWARF CUCUMBER
Cucumis sativus 'Midget Cucumber'

the two to three months that midget melons need to mature, sow seeds indoors or in a hotbed three to four weeks before plants go into the garden. Elsewhere, sow seeds outdoors after the soil has warmed.

Prepare a hill for planting by digging a hole 1 foot deep and 2 feet across. Trowel a 4- to 6-inch layer of compost and a 1- to 2-inch layer of peat moss into the bottom of the hole. Replace the topsoil to form a mound. Hills should be spaced 4 feet apart. Plant six to eight seeds in a circle a foot in diameter on top of each hill; thin seedlings to the two strongest when each one has developed a pair of true leaves (not the seed leaves that appear first). Water the vines well. A mulch of hay or straw conserves moisture, helps prevent the melons from rotting and minimizes cultivation around the shallow roots and fragile vines. Pick watermelons when an early morning rap on the fruit produces a deep, dull thud.

CUCUMIS
C. melo hybrids (dwarf cantaloupe or muskmelon), *C. sativus* hybrids (dwarf cucumber)

The sprawling vines of full-sized cantaloupes and cucumbers ordinarily bar these two edibles from small gardens. Dwarf varieties have changed that.

Dwarf cantaloupes no larger than softballs ripen in 60 to 65 days on vines only 3 or 4 feet long. Minnesota Midget and Farnorth are two varieties that have the sweet orange flesh of standard-sized melons.

Dwarf cucumbers grow on vines 2 to 3 feet long that will climb a fence or other support. Mini, Midget and Tiny Dill varieties start producing numerous 3- to 4-inch cucumbers in 55 days on vines 2 feet long or less. They are all slicing cucumbers, best when eaten raw.

HOW TO GROW. Cantaloupes and cucumbers grow best in light, sandy soil. A soil with a neutral pH suits either one, and cucumbers will also grow well in slightly acid soils. Both need warm night temperatures, 55° or higher, and day temperatures of 80° or above. In regions where these temperatures are expected for less than three months, sow seeds indoors one month before the plants can be set in the garden. Elsewhere, sow seeds outdoors after frost danger has passed.

Plant cantaloupes and cucumbers in hills prepared by digging holes 1 foot deep and 2 feet across. Put a 4-inch layer of compost and about a cupful of cottonseed meal into the bottom of each hole. Replace the topsoil to form a mound. Space these hills about 3 feet apart. Plant about six seeds ½ inch deep in a 12-inch circle on the top of each hill. When seedlings appear, remove all but two or three of the strongest. If you are growing cucumbers as climbing plants, space plants 10 to 12 inches apart. Both cantaloupes and cucumbers need the equivalent of 1 inch of rain each week to grow well. A mulch of hay or straw underneath the vines conserves moisture, prevents fruits from rotting, and minimizes cultivation around the shallow roots and fragile vines.

Pick cantaloupes when a slight pressure at the point where stem and melon join causes the melon to break away from the vine. Cut cucumbers from the vine when they turn dark green or even before they reach that stage. Do not let cucumbers stay on the vine past maturity; if cucumbers turn yellow and start going to seed, the vines will stop producing.

CORN See *Zea*
CUCUMBER See *Cucumis*

CUCURBITA
C. maxima hybrids (miniature winter squash), *C. pepo* hybrids (miniature pumpkin)

Though the sprawling vines of standard-sized pumpkins and winter squashes need plenty of space to spread, miniature and dwarf varieties that grow either as bushes or compact vines make it possible to include some of these vegetables in small gardens.

Miniature and dwarf winter squashes are as flavorful and suitable for winter storage as are the standard-sized varieties. Gold Nugget and Kindred are bush-type squashes that grow about 30 inches tall and 3 to 4 feet wide with 2- to 3-pound fruits that resemble little pumpkins. Eat-All has compact, 5-foot vines that bear 5-inch fruits that somewhat resemble tiny watermelons. These winter squashes mature in about 90 days. Butterbush bears 1½-pound yellow to orange fruits in about one fourth the space required by butternut squash vines; it matures in 75 days.

Among the miniature pumpkin varieties available, Cinderella produces fruits up to 7 pounds in weight on bushy plants that take up only 6 square feet of space. Spirit is a compact, semibush variety that spreads about 5 feet in diameter; its bright orange oval fruits weigh 10 to 15 pounds. These bush pumpkin varieties mature in about 100 days. Good dwarf vine varieties are Small Sugar, which has fine-grained flesh that is excellent for pies, and Jack O'Lantern. Vine-type pumpkins need 110 to 115 days for their 10- to 15-pound fruits to reach maturity.

HOW TO GROW. Winter squashes and pumpkins grow best in full sun, although pumpkins can grow in partial shade. Start seeds indoors one week before the last killing frost and set the seedlings out two weeks later, or sow the seeds outdoors when night temperatures stay about 55°. Prepare hills in the garden by digging holes 1 to 1½ feet deep and 2 feet wide, mixing a 4-inch layer of compost and about a cupful of cottonseed meal into the bottom of the hole; then replace the topsoil to form a gently sloping mound. Plant six to eight seeds in a circle around the top of the mound or set in three or four previously started seedlings, being careful to avoid disturbing the roots. Provide ample water. A thick mulch of straw or hay conserves moisture, reduces weeding and helps to keep fruits from rotting. When pumpkin leaves have withered or winter squash skins are extremely hard, cut the fruits from the vine, taking a 2- to 3-inch stem. Allow fruits to harden for about 10 days, putting them in the sun but off the ground, then store in a cool, dry place.

DAUCUS
D. carota hybrids (dwarf carrot)

Finger-length dwarf carrots are sweeter and have smaller cores than full-sized varieties. Their main advantage in a small garden is that they do not require soil beds that have been prepared as deeply as beds for longer carrots. Narrow, 3-inch Baby Finger Nantes is most tender if it is harvested before it fully matures, about 50 days after planting. Little Finger, 4 inches long, and Tiny Sweet, 3 inches long, are both stubby, cone-shaped carrots almost 2 inches wide at the top; they mature in 65 days. Konfrix is so short and plump that it resembles an orange radish; it matures in 65 days.

HOW TO GROW. Carrots grow best in loose, sandy soil. The bed should be free of rocks or tree roots that the sensitive carrots would twist and fork to avoid. Carrots grow best in full sun, though they tolerate dappled shade. They do not grow well if the temperature exceeds 90°; day temperatures between 40° and 80° are ideal.

Sow seeds one month before the last spring frost or as soon as the soil can be worked, and make successive sowings at three-week intervals until early summer. Another sowing can be made two months before the first fall frost for a final crop.

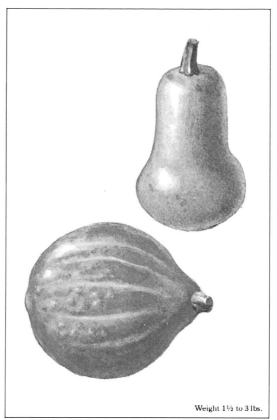

Weight 1½ to 3 lbs.

MINIATURE WINTER SQUASHES
Cucurbita maxima hybrids

Weight 10 to 15 lbs.

MINIATURE PUMPKIN
Cucurbita pepo 'Small Sugar'

For climate zones, see map, page 151.

House plants, page 123;   Orchids, page 131;   Rock garden plants, page 134;   Roses, page 143;   Vegetables and fruits, page 145.

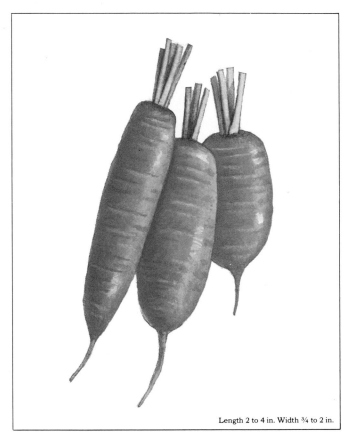

Length 2 to 4 in. Width ¾ to 2 in.

DWARF CARROTS
Daucus carota hybrids

Diameter ¹¹⁄₁₆ in. Mound 4 to 6 in.

ALPINE STRAWBERRY
Fragaria vesca semperflorens 'Baron Solemacher'

Sow carrot seeds ½ inch deep in rows 12 inches apart. Cover the seeds with a light layer of vermiculite, sifted compost or grass clippings to prevent the soil from forming a crust that would prevent the tiny seedlings from breaking through the surface. As seedlings appear, thin them so the plants are an inch apart. When the carrots are about ½ inch in diameter, pull every other plant. The final fall crop can be stored in the ground for the winter if you cover it with a 6-inch mulch of hay, straw or grass clippings after frost has killed the tops.

EGGPLANT See *Solanum*

FRAGARIA
F. vesca semperflorens (alpine strawberry)

Unlike other strawberries, alpine strawberries grow in neat clumps and do not send out runners. Forming 6- to 8-inch mounds of tooth-edged green leaves, these perennials are used as low border plants as well as being grown for their flavorful tiny berries. Baron Solemacher is a variety with ½-inch white flowers followed by a continuous crop of red dime-sized berries that can be eaten or left to hang ornamentally on the erect stems.

HOW TO GROW. Alpine strawberries grow best in acid soil, pH 5.8 to 6.5, that has been supplemented with compost or dried manure. They thrive in full sun but will grow in partial shade. Sow seeds outdoors after the last spring frost, planting them ½ inch deep and 2 inches apart. Seeds can also be started indoors six to eight weeks before the last frost and transplanted outdoors as soon as the ground can be worked. Plants started indoors may bear fruit the first summer; plants grown outdoors from seed usually require two seasons to fruit. Newly started plants of Baron Solemacher are available from some nurseries.

LETTUCE See *Lactuca*

LACTUCA
L. sativa hybrids (dwarf lettuce)

Succulent dwarf lettuce provides a crop for your salad bowl from the time its seedlings first appear in the garden. Seedlings thinned from rows are delicious, and tender leaves can be cut at any time while the lettuce is growing. Two small varieties, Tom Thumb and Summer Bibb, are both butterhead types with leaves that form loose heads with green outer layers and a pale-green-to-yellow core.

Tom Thumb is a true miniature with a compact head the size of a tennis ball; it matures in 65 days. Single heads are sometimes used as individual salads. Summer Bibb is slightly smaller than standard Bibb lettuce. It is only 8 to 10 inches across when it matures in 60 days, though it is most tender before the heads reach full size.

HOW TO GROW. Lettuce grows best in mildly acid soil with a pH of 6.0 to 7.0. It is a cool-weather crop that goes to seed when temperatures average 80° or more during the day. Plant lettuce in full sun in spring and fall, in partial shade during the hottest part of the summer. Prepare the soil by digging in compost and ¼ to ½ pound of 5-10-5 garden fertilizer for every 10-foot row.

Seeds can be started indoors a month before the last spring frost and transplanted outdoors when the seedlings are 2 to 3 inches tall and night temperatures remain above 25°. Seeds can be sown directly in the garden as soon as the soil can be worked in spring. Space seedlings 6 inches apart in rows 1½ feet apart. Successive sowings can be made at two-week intervals as long as temperatures will be cool enough for the crop to mature. Provide the equivalent of at least 1 inch of rain each week but avoid wetting the leaves more than necessary. If you harvest lettuce by cutting the leaves from the plants rather than pulling the plants out by their roots, a second crop may grow. The compact varieties also can be grown in window boxes or planters.

LYCOPERSICON
L. esculentum hybrids (miniature or dwarf tomato)

A number of miniature and dwarf varieties of tomato are available, some developed specifically for growing in pots. These small tomatoes are threatened by the same diseases that can devastate standard-sized tomatoes, so you should be sure to select disease-resistant varieties.

Tiny Tim is a true miniature. The bushy plant grows only 8 inches tall and about 15 inches wide. It begins producing tiny, ¾-inch tomatoes 45 days after seedlings are planted outdoors and may bear more than 200 fruits per plant. Recommended for pot culture, both yellow- and red-fruited varieties are available. Pixie is a fast-growing dwarf plant, 18 inches tall or less, that bears 2-inch red tomatoes in 52 days. It was developed for pot or window-box growing. Pear and Plum tomatoes grow on dwarf plants 15 to 24 inches tall; the yellow or red pear-shaped or oblong fruits are about 2 inches long and an inch in diameter. They mature in 70 days. Patio hybrids grow 24 to 30 inches tall and begin producing bright red 2- to 3-inch tomatoes in 50 days. Small Fry grows 30 to 40 inches tall with clusters of 1-inch red fruits in 52 days.

HOW TO GROW. Tomatoes grow best in acid soils with a pH of 5.5 to 6.5 and need as much direct sun as you can give them—at least six hours daily. Since tomatoes are warm-season plants that cannot be grown outdoors until all danger of frost has passed, most gardeners set out purchased plants or start seeds indoors. Sow seeds ⅛ inch deep five to seven weeks before night temperatures are expected to stay above 60°. When the seedlings are 1 inch tall, transplant them to individual 3 inch pots. Prepare the soil bed by digging in 1½ pounds of 5-10-5 fertilizer for every 25 feet of row or ¼ ounce per gallon container. When night temperatures stay above 60°, set plants in the garden, spacing all varieties except Tiny Tim 2 feet apart in rows 2 feet apart; Tiny Tim can be planted at intervals of 1 foot. All of these varieties need to be staked.

Fertilize the plants once a month by scattering a handful of 5-10-5 fertilizer around each plant, then watering thoroughly to carry the plant food down to the roots. Provide ample water to keep the soil moist at all times, especially for container-grown plants. To encourage the tomatoes to set fruit rather than grow foliage, prune away any side shoots that grow in the joints where the leaves join the main stem.

Harvest tomatoes when they have developed their full color, lifting them gently until the stem snaps. If frost threatens while nearly ripe fruits are still on the plants, remove them and ripen them indoors in a single layer at 65°.

MUSKMELON See *Cucumis*

PUMPKIN See *Cucurbita*

SOLANUM
S. melongena 'Morden Midget' (dwarf eggplant)

Morden Midget is a dwarf variety of the bushy eggplant which, with its shiny purple fruits, is one of the most ornamental of vegetables. This variety grows no more than 2 feet tall and produces three to six medium-sized fruits per bush in about 65 days. These can be eaten when only 3 inches long, or harvested when they reach their full 6-inch size. Morden

For climate zones, see map, page 151.

Diameter 2 in.

MINIATURE LETTUCE
Lactuca sativa 'Tom Thumb'

Diameter ¾ to 3 in. Height 8 to 15 in.

MINIATURE AND DWARF TOMATOES
Lycopersicon esculentum hybrids

House plants, page 123;   Orchids, page 131;   Rock garden plants, page 134;   Roses, page 143;   Vegetables and fruits, page 145.

Length 3 to 6 in. Height 2 ft.

DWARF EGGPLANT
Solanum melongena 'Morden Midget'

Length 4 to 6 in. Height 2 to 3 ft.

DWARF SWEET CORN
Zea mays 'Golden Midget'

Midget is one of the first eggplants to mature and grows well in a tub or planter.

HOW TO GROW. Eggplant needs a long, hot summer—at least 2½ months of night temperatures above 55°, rising to 80° or higher in the daytime. Buy plants that are already started or sow seeds ½ inch deep indoors 8 to 10 weeks before the plants will be set outdoors. When the seedlings are 1 to 1½ inches tall, transplant them to 3- or 4-inch pots. Keep the plants warm and moist so growth continues unchecked. Eggplant grows best in acid soil, pH 5.5 to 6.5, in full sun. When night temperatures stay above 55°, set plants outside, spacing them 2 feet apart in rows 3 feet apart. Prepare the soil bed by digging in a generous layer of compost. Give each plant 1 pint of a water-soluble fertilizer such as fish emulsion diluted to one half the strength recommended on the label. Fertilize the plants again in four to six weeks by scattering ¼ cup of 5-10-5 fertilizer in a 1½-foot band around each plant. Water whenever rainfall is less than 1 inch in a week.

When a dent made by pressing a finger firmly against the fruit's skin remains, the eggplant is mature. You may harvest and eat eggplants before they are ripe, but if they are left on the bush past maturity, the plant will stop producing.

SQUASH See *Cucurbita*
STRAWBERRY See *Fragaria*
SWEET CORN See *Zea*

TOMATO See *Lycopersicon*

WATERMELON See *Citrullus*

ZEA
Z. mays hybrids (dwarf sweet corn)

The delicate flavor of fresh sweet corn plucked from the plant and plunged directly into the cooking pot is an elusive gastronomic delight. This is reason enough to grow sweet corn in a tiny garden, but dwarf varieties have advantages other than small size. Midget corn varieties grow fast and their ears are a convenient size to freeze for corn on the cob in winter. They produce from two to five ears of corn 4 to 6 inches long on each stalk 2 to 3 feet tall in about 60 days. Golden Midget and Midget Hybrid are yellow varieties; White Midget bears white-kerneled ears.

HOW TO GROW. Sweet corn grows best in full sun in soil with a pH of 5.8 to 6.8. In Zones 3-8, sow seeds outdoors two weeks after the last spring frost. In Zones 9 and 10, sow seeds whenever temperatures can be expected to stay between 40° at night and 85° during the day for two months. For successive crops, sow seeds every two weeks until three months before the first fall frost or until temperatures will no longer stay in the ideal range.

Since corn is pollinated by wind-borne pollen, sow seeds in blocks of four short rows or hills 2 feet apart. Plant the seeds 1 inch deep in the spring when the soil is relatively moist, 2 inches deep during drier summer weather. Plant seeds 2 to 3 inches apart in rows or plant six seeds per hill; thin seedlings to stand 6 inches apart in rows, or three plants per hill.

Prepare the soil for corn by spading a 4-inch layer of compost and about a cup of a garden fertilizer such as 5-10-5 into the soil for each 5 feet of row; the plants in enriched soil will not require further feeding. Water if plants show signs of wilting, especially when tassels appear and ears are forming. A mulch of hay or straw conserves moisture around the shallow roots. Pick corn when the ears feel full and firm and the silk tassels turn brown.

For climate zones, see map, page 151.

Appendix

Survival zones for small plants

Because their root structures are so shallow and fine, miniature and dwarf plants that are grown outdoors need special care in winter. This protection begins at the most elementary level: in the selection of plants that are hardy enough to survive the minimum winter temperature expected where you live. That is why each entry in the encyclopedia that begins on page 98 is keyed to the climate zones on the map below.

Within these zones, however, average temperatures vary, depending on such regional factors as the altitude at which your garden grows, or the closeness of an ocean or one of the Great Lakes that moderates the temperature of the land surrounding it. The records of your local weather bureau are your best guide to the precise climate of your immediate area.

Even within a safe temperature zone, small plants may need more protection than their larger relatives: a winter mulch to keep their roots moist and uniformly cold, regardless of alternate thawing and freezing temperatures; a screen to shade their foliage from winter sunscald; a windbreak to temper fierce winter winds. In regions where the winter temperatures are mild, torrential rain could easily wash away an entire garden of miniature plants, whose roothold in the earth is fragile at best, unless the plants are sheltered with a rain shield or a barrier is provided to direct the flow of water away from them.

If you decide to move your indoor plants out to the terrace or the garden for the summer months, condition them gradually to bright sunlight so they do not get sunburned.

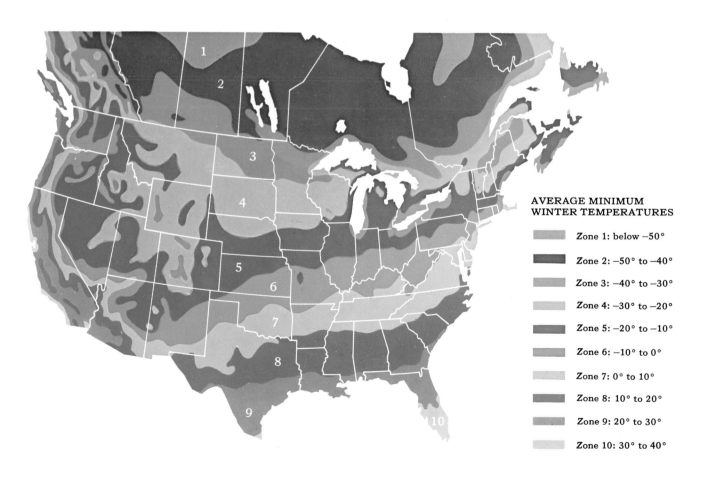

AVERAGE MINIMUM
WINTER TEMPERATURES

Zone 1: below −50°

Zone 2: −50° to −40°

Zone 3: −40° to −30°

Zone 4: −30° to −20°

Zone 5: −20° to −10°

Zone 6: −10° to 0°

Zone 7: 0° to 10°

Zone 8: 10° to 20°

Zone 9: 20° to 30°

Zone 10: 30° to 40°

Characteristics of 117 miniatures

Listed below for quick reference are the species illustrated in Chapter 5.

	MATURE HEIGHT				GROWTH HABIT				USES						SPECIAL TRAITS					SOIL			LIGHT	
	Under 6 inches	6 to 12 inches	1 to 3 feet	Over 3 feet	Upright	Spreading	Trailing	Climbing	Potted house plant	Terrarium	Dish garden	Rock garden	Bed or border	Garden specimen	Flowers	Distinctive foliage	Evergreen	Decorative fruit	Edible fruit	Dry	Moist	Wet	Bright light	Indirect light
ACER PALMATUM 'DISSECTUM' (threadleaf Japanese maple)			●	●	●							●		●		●				●			●	
ADIANTUM RENIFORME (maidenhair fern)		●			●				●	●		●				●				●				●
ALOE DESCOINGSII (miniature aloe)	●				●				●	●	●			●				●		●			●	
ANACYCLUS DEPRESSUS (Atlas daisy)	●				●							●		●				●		●			●	
ANEMONE BLANDA 'RADAR' (Greek anemone)	●				●						●	●		●				●		●			●	●
AQUILEGIA FLABELLATA PUMILA (fan columbine)	●				●	●					●	●		●						●			●	
ARUNDINARIA PYGMAEA (dwarf bamboo)		●			●				●						●	●				●			●	
ASPLENIUM EBENOIDES (Scott's spleenwort)	●				●			●	●							●				●				●
AZOLLA FILICULOIDES (mosquito fern)	●					●			●							●						●	●	
BEGONIA BOGNERI (grass-leaf begonia)	●				●				●	●					●	●				●				●
BRASSICA OLERACEA CAPITATA 'DWARF MORDEN' (miniature cabbage)	●				●						●			●					●		●		●	
BROWALLIA SPECIOSA MAJOR 'BLUE TROLL' (blue troll browallia)	●					●			●		●	●		●						●				●
BUXUS MICROPHYLLA 'COMPACTA' (Kingsville dwarf boxwood)		●			●	●			●					●			●			●			●	
CAMPANULA ELATINES GARGANICA (Adriatic bellflower)	●					●	●				●	●		●						●				●
CATTLEYA WALKERANA (dwarf cattleya orchid)		●			●				●					●				●		●				●
CHAMAECYPARIS OBTUSA 'NANA GRACILIS' (dwarf false cypress)			●	●							●			●		●	●			●			●	
CHIONODOXA SARDENSIS (glory-of-the-snow)	●				●					●	●	●		●						●			●	
CITRULLUS LANATUS 'NEW HAMPSHIRE MIDGET' (miniature watermelon)			●			●					●							●	●	●			●	
CITRUS AURANTIUM MYRTIFOLIA (myrtle-leaf orange)			●	●					●		●	●	●	●		●	●	●	●	●			●	
COMPARETTIA FALCATA (dwarf comparettia orchid)		●			●				●					●						●				●
CROCUS VERSICOLOR (spring-flowering crocus)	●				●					●	●	●		●						●			●	
CROCUS ZONATUS (autumn-flowering crocus)	●				●					●	●	●		●						●			●	
CRYPTOMERIA JAPONICA 'GLOBOSA NANA' (dwarf Japanese cedar)		●	●	●	●						●		●			●	●			●			●	
CUCUMIS MELO 'MINNESOTA MIDGET' (dwarf cantaloupe)			●			●		●			●								●	●			●	
CUCUMIS SATIVUS 'MIDGET CUCUMBER' (dwarf cucumber)			●			●	●	●			●								●	●			●	
CUCURBITA MAXIMA HYBRIDS (miniature winter squashes)			●			●					●								●	●			●	
CUCURBITA PEPO 'SMALL SUGAR' (miniature pumpkin)			●			●					●								●	●		●	●	
DAHLIA HYBRID 'BRIGHT SPOT' (formal decorative dahlia)			●	●							●		●							●	●		●	
DAHLIA HYBRID 'IDA LOIS' (straight cactus dahlia)			●	●							●		●							●	●		●	
DAHLIA HYBRID 'NEPOS' (waterlily dahlia)			●	●							●		●							●	●		●	
DAHLIA HYBRID 'POM OF POMS' (pompon dahlia)			●	●							●		●							●	●		●	
DAUCUS CAROTA HYBRIDS (dwarf carrots)	●				●			●			●							●	●			●		
DENDROBIUM JENKINSII (dwarf dendrobium orchid)	●				●				●					●						●				●
DIANTHUS ALPINUS (alpine pink)	●				●							●	●	●		●	●			●				●
DRABA MOLLISSIMA	●			●							●		●	●	●	●				●				●
ECHEVERIA MINIMA (miniature hen-and-chickens)	●				●				●	●								●		●			●	
EDRAIANTHUS PUMILIO (grassy bells)	●				●						●	●	●	●						●			●	
EPISCIA DIANTHIFLORA (flame violet)	●					●	●		●	●				●						●				●
EQUISETUM SCIRPOIDES (dwarf scouring rush)	●				●	●			●	●					●	●					●	●		●
ERYTHRONIUM 'PAGODA' (pagoda fawn lily)		●			●						●	●		●						●			●	
FICUS PUMILA 'MINIMA' (miniature climbing fig)	●					●	●	●	●	●				●		●				●				●
FITTONIA VERSHAFELTII ARGYRONEURA 'MINIMA' (dwarf silver-veined fittonia)	●					●	●		●	●						●				●				●
FRAGARIA VESCA SEMPERFLORENS 'BARON SOLEMACHER' (alpine strawberry)		●			●							●	●					●	●		●		●	
FRAILEA GRAHLIANA	●				●				●	●	●				●					●			●	
FRITILLARIA MELEAGRIS (checkered fritillary)		●			●						●	●		●						●			●	
GALANTHUS NIVALIS (common snowdrop)	●	●			●						●	●		●						●			●	
GARDENIA JASMINOIDES VEITCHII (dwarf gardenia)			●		●				●			●	●		●					●			●	
GENTIANA ACAULIS (stemless gentian)	●				●						●		●							●			●	
GERANIUM SANGUINEUM PROSTRATUM (crane's-bill)	●				●		●				●	●		●	●			●		●			●	
GESNERIA CHRISTII		●			●				●	●				●						●				●
GLADIOLUS HORTULANUS (miniature gladiolus)			●		●						●		●							●			●	

	MATURE HEIGHT				GROWTH HABIT				USES								SPECIAL TRAITS			SOIL			LIGHT	
	Under 6 inches	6 to 12 inches	1 to 3 feet	Over 3 feet	Upright	Spreading	Trailing	Climbing	Potted house plant	Terrarium	Dish garden	Rock garden	Bed or border	Garden specimen	Flowers	Distinctive foliage	Evergreen	Decorative fruit	Edible fruit	Dry	Moist	Wet	Bright light	Indirect light
GRAPTOPETALUM MACDOUGALLII	●				●				●		●				●					●			●	●
GYMNOCALYCIUM BRUCHII (Bruch's chin cactus)	●				●				●						●					●			●	
GYPSOPHILA REPENS 'FRATENSIS' (creeping babies'-breath)	●				●	●			●						●	●				●			●	
HEDERA HELIX 'JUBILEE' (miniature English ivy)	●					●	●	●	●	●	●					●	●				●			●
HEDERA HELIX 'MERION BEAUTY' (miniature English ivy)	●					●	●	●	●	●	●					●	●				●			●
HUERNIA PILLANSII (cocklebur)	●				●				●						●					●				●
ILEX CRENATA 'DWARF PAGODA' (dwarf pagoda holly)		●			●				●		●				●	●	●				●		●	●
IRIS DANFORDIAE (danford iris)	●				●							●			●						●		●	
JUNIPERUS CHINENSIS 'ECHINIFORMIS' (hedgehog juniper)			●		●				●			●	●	●		●	●				●		●	
KOELLIKERIA ERINOIDES	●	●			●				●						●						●			●
LACTUCA SATIVA 'TOM THUMB' (miniature lettuce)	●				●				●				●						●		●		●	
LEMMAPHYLLUM MICROPHYLLUM	●						●		●	●						●					●			●
LINUM ELEGANS 'GEMMELL'S HYBRID' (dwarf flowering flax)		●			●				●	●					●			●			●		●	
LOBULARIA MARITIMA 'VIOLET QUEEN' (dwarf sweet alyssum)	●					●			●	●					●			●			●		●	
LYCOPERSICON ESCULENTUM HYBRIDS (miniature and dwarf tomatoes)		●			●				●						●				●		●		●	
MAMMILLARIA PROLIFERA (silver-cluster cactus)	●				●				●	●	●				●			●		●			●	
MASDEVALLIA LILLIPUTIANA (miniature masdevallia orchid)	●				●				●						●						●			●
NARCISSUS BULBOCODIUM CONSPICUUS (petticoat daffodil)	●				●				●				●		●						●		●	●
NARCISSUS CANALICULATUS		●			●				●			●	●		●						●		●	●
NARCISSUS CYCLAMINEUS (cyclamen-flowered daffodil)	●				●				●			●	●		●						●		●	●
NARCISSUS CYCLAMINEUS 'TETE-A-TETE' (tete-a-tete daffodil)		●			●				●			●	●		●						●		●	●
NARCISSUS PUMILIS PLENUS 'RIP VAN WINKLE'		●			●				●			●	●		●						●		●	●
NARCISSUS TRIANDUS ALBUS (angel's tears daffodil)		●			●				●			●	●		●						●		●	●
NEOFINETIA FALCATA (samurai orchid)	●				●				●						●						●			●
ORNITHOGALUM UMBELLATUM (common star-of-Bethlehem)		●			●	●			●			●	●		●						●		●	●
PELARGONIUM HORTORUM 'BLACK VESUVIUS' (miniature common geranium)	●				●				●			●	●		●	●					●		●	
PELARGONIUM PELTATUM 'SUGAR BABY' (miniature ivy geranium)	●				●				●			●	●		●	●					●		●	
PEPEROMIA COLUMELLA (columnar peperomia)	●				●				●	●	●					●				●				●
PICEA PUNGENS 'GLAUCA PROCUMBENS' (grafted dwarf Colorado blue spruce)		●				●						●		●		●	●				●		●	
PILEA CADIEREI 'MINIMA' (dwarf aluminum plant)	●				●				●							●					●			●
PINUS MUGO 'MOPS' (dwarf mugo pine)			●		●							●		●		●	●				●		●	
PRIMULA MARGINATA (silver-edged primrose)	●				●							●	●		●						●		●	
PSEUDOTSUGA MENZIESII 'DENSA' (dwarf Douglas fir)			●		●							●		●		●	●				●		●	
QUERCIFILIX ZEILANICA (oak fern)	●	●			●	●				●						●					●		●	
REBUTIA ALBIFLORA (white crown cactus)	●				●	●			●		●	●			●			●		●			●	
RHODODENDRON FORRESTII REPENS (dwarf rhododendron)	●					●						●	●		●		●				●			●
RHODODENDRON RADICANS (dwarf rhododendron)	●				●							●	●		●		●				●			●
RHODODENDRON KIUSIANUM (dwarf azalea)		●			●							●	●		●		●				●		●	
RHODODENDRON NAKAHARAI (dwarf azalea)		●			●							●	●		●		●				●		●	
ROSA HYBRID 'KARA' (miniature rose)		●			●				●			●	●		●						●		●	
ROSA HYBRID 'LAVENDER LACE' (miniature rose)			●		●				●			●	●		●						●		●	
ROSA HYBRID 'RED CASCADE' (miniature rose)		●					●	●	●				●		●						●		●	
ROSA HYBRID 'RISE 'N' SHINE' (miniature rose)		●			●				●				●		●						●		●	
ROSA HYBRID 'SIMPLEX' (miniature rose)		●			●				●				●		●						●		●	
ROSA HYBRID 'STARINA' (miniature rose)		●	●		●				●			●	●		●						●		●	
SAINTPAULIA 'LITTLE RASCAL' (miniature African violet)	●				●				●	●					●						●			●
SAINTPAULIA 'WEE LASS' (miniature African violet)	●				●				●	●					●						●	●		●
SALIX RETICULATA (depressed willow)	●				●							●			●	●					●		●	●
SAXIFRAGA KABSCHIA 'FERDINANDI-COBURGI' (saxifrage)	●				●							●			●					●				●
SINNINGIA PUSILLA (miniature sinningia)	●				●				●	●					●						●			●
SINNINGIA PUSILLA 'WHITE SPRITE' (miniature sinningia)	●	●			●				●	●					●						●			●

153

	MATURE HEIGHT				GROWTH HABIT				USES						SPECIAL TRAITS					SOIL			LIGHT	
	Under 6 inches	6 to 12 inches	1 to 3 feet	Over 3 feet	Upright	Spreading	Trailing	Climbing	Potted house plant	Terrarium	Dish garden	Rock garden	Bed or border	Garden specimen	Flowers	Distinctive foliage	Evergreen	Decorative fruit	Edible fruit	Dry	Moist	Wet	Bright light	Indirect light
SOLANUM MELONGENA 'MORDEN MIDGET' (dwarf eggplant)		●	●								●		●						●	●	●			
SOLEIROLIA SOLEIROLII (baby's tears)	●			●			●		●	●	●	●				●					●			●
SOPHRONITELLA VIOLACEA (dwarf sophronitella orchid)	●				●				●			●			●						●			●
STREPTOCARPUS 'CAPE BEAUTY' (Cape primrose)	●				●				●	●		●	●								●			●
TAGETES PATULA NANA 'DAINTY MARIETTA' (dwarf French marigold)		●			●	●					●	●		●							●			
THUJA OCCIDENTALIS 'RHEINGOLD' (dwarf American arborvitae)			●	●	●						●		●			●	●			●	●			
THYMUS PSEUDOLANUGINOSUS (woolly thyme)	●					●	●				●	●				●					●			
TSUGA CANADENSIS 'COLE' (dwarf Canadian hemlock)	●										●	●					●			●	●			
TULIPA KOLPAKOWSKIANA (miniature tulip)	●				●						●	●		●						●	●			
TULIPA PULCHELLA (miniature tulip)	●				●						●	●		●							●			
TULIPA PULCHELLA 'VIOLACEA' (miniature tulip)	●				●						●	●		●							●			
TULIPA TARDA (miniature tulip)	●				●						●	●		●					●		●			
VIOLA TRICOLOR 'HEARTSEASE' (wild pansy)	●				●						●	●		●						●	●	●		
ZEA MAYS 'GOLDEN MIDGET' (dwarf sweet corn)		●	●								●							●		●	●			

Picture credits

The sources for the illustrations in this book are listed below. Credits from left to right are separated by semicolons, from top to bottom by dashes. Cover: Richard Jeffery. 4: Philip Perl. 6: Richard Jeffery. 10 through 16: Drawings by Joan McGurren. 19 through 22: John Neubauer. 23: John Neubauer, except top left, Tom Tracy. 24, 25, 26: John Neubauer. 29 through 34: Drawings by Kathy Rebeiz. 37 through 48: Richard Jeffery. 52: Drawing by Joan McGurren. 55: Drawing by Kathy Rebeiz. 59: Richard Jeffery. 60: John Neubauer. 61: Richard Jeffery. 62, 63: Richard Weymouth Brooks. 64: Entheos, except top right, Richard Weymouth Brooks. 65: Entheos. 66: Tom Tracy, designed by John Y. Naka. 68: Drawing by Joan McGurren. 70 through 78: Drawings by Kathy Rebeiz. 81: John Y. Naka, designed by John Y. Naka. 82: Tom Tracy, designed by John Y. Naka. 83: Tom Tracy, designed by John Y. Naka—Tom Tracy, designed by Ben Oki; Bernard Askienazy, designed by Jerald P. Stowell. 84: All Bernard Askienazy, top and bottom left, designed by Jerald P. Stowell. 85: Bernard Askienazy. 86, 87, 88: Tom Tracy, designed by Ben Oki. 89: Bernard Askienazy, designed by Jerald P. Stowell. 90: Bernard Askienazy. 91: Tom Tracy, designed by John Y. Naka—Bernard Askienazy, designed by Jerald P. Stowell. 92: Bernard Askienazy. 93: Bernard Askienazy, designed by Jerald P. Stowell. 94: Bernard Askienazy, designed by Doris W. Froning. 95: Bernard Askienazy. 96 through 150: Artists for encyclopedia illustrations listed in alphabetical order: Adolph E. Brotman, Richard Crist, Forte, Inc., Susan M. Johnston, Mary Kellner, Gwen Leighton and Eduardo Salgado. 151: Map by Adolph E. Brotman.

Bibliography

Aoki, Kotaro, *Nyumon Shumi no Bonsai*. Hikarinokuni, Inc., Osaka, 1977.

Ashberry, Anne, *Miniature Gardens*. David & Charles, 1977.

Ashberry, Anne, *Miniature Trees and Shrubs*. Nicholas Kaye, Ltd., 1958.

Bailey, L. H., *Standard Cyclopedia of Horticulture*. The Macmillan Co., 1935.

Baur, Robert C., *Gardens in Glass Containers*. Hearthside Press, 1960.

Behme, Robert Lee, *Bonsai, Saikei and Bonkei: Japanese Dwarf Trees and Tray Landscapes*. William Morrow & Co., Inc., 1969.

Brilmayer, Bernice, *All About Miniature Plants and Gardens Indoors and Out*. Doubleday & Co., Inc., 1963.

Britton, Nathaniel L., and Rose, J. N., *The Cactaceae: Descriptions and Illustrations of Plants of the Cactus Family*. Dover Publications, Inc., 1963.

Brooklyn Botanic Garden, *Dwarf Conifers: A Handbook on Low and Slow-Growing Evergreens*. BBG, 1977.

Brooklyn Botanic Garden, *Handbook on African Violets and Their Relatives*. BBG, 1967.

Brooklyn Botanic Garden, *Handbook on Dwarfed Potted Trees*. BBG, 1977.

Brooklyn Botanic Garden, *Handbook on Miniature Gardens*. BBG, 1972.

Chittenden, Fred J., ed., *The Royal Horticultural Society Dictionary of Gardening*, 2nd ed. Clarendon Press, 1974.

Cox, Peter A., *Dwarf Rhododendrons*. Macmillan, 1973.

Elbert, George A., *The Indoor Light Gardening Book*. Crown Publishers, Inc., 1973.

Elbert, Virginie F. and George A., *The Miracle Houseplants*. Crown Publishers, Inc., 1976.

Fitch, Charles Marden, *The Complete Book of Miniature Roses*. Hawthorn Books, Inc., 1977.

Genders, Roy, *Gardening in Miniature*. Robert Hale, Ltd., 1958.

Genders, Roy, *Miniature Bulbs*. St. Martin's Press, 1963.

Griffith, Anna N., *A Guide to Rock Garden Plants*. E. P.

Dutton & Co., Inc., 1964.

Hawkes, Alex D., *Encyclopedia of Cultivated Orchids.* Faber and Faber, Ltd., 1965.

Haworth, James P., *Plant Magic.* Binfords and Mort, 1946.

Hills, Lawrence D., *Alpines without a Garden.* Faber and Faber, Ltd., 1953.

Hoshizaki, Barbara Joe, *Fern Growers Manual.* Alfred A. Knopf, Inc., 1975.

Hume, Harold, *Hollies.* The Macmillan Co., 1953.

Iwasa, Ryoji, *Bonsai Bunka-shi.* Yasaka Shobo, Tokyo, 1976.

Kawasumi, Masakuni, *Introductory Bonsai.* Japan Publications, 1970.

Lawrence, Elizabeth, *The Little Bulbs.* Criterion Books, 1975.

McDonald, Elvin, *Little Plants for Small Spaces.* M. Evans & Co., 1975.

McDonald, Elvin, *Miniature Plants for Home and Greenhouse.* D. Van Nostrand Co., Inc., 1962.

Matthew, Brian, *Dwarf Bulbs.* Arco Publishing Co., Inc., 1973.

Naka, John Yoshio, *Bonsai Techniques.* Dennis-Landman, 1973.

Nakajima, Tameji, and Young, H. Carl, *The Art of the Chrysanthemum.* Harper & Row, 1965.

Nakamura, Zeko, *Komono Bonsai.* Shufunotomo-sha, Tokyo, 1973.

Northen, Rebecca Tyson, *Home Orchid Growing,* rev. ed. Van Nostrand Reinhold Co., 1970.

Pierot, Suzanne, *The Ivy Book.* The Macmillan Co., 1974.

Pipe, Ann K., *Bonsai: The Art of Dwarfing Trees.* Hawthorn Books, Inc., 1964.

Schroeder, Marion, *The Green Thumb Directory.* Doubleday & Co., Inc., 1977.

Staff of the L. H. Bailey Hortorium, Cornell University, *Hortus Third: A Dictionary of Plants Cultivated in the United States and Canada.* Macmillan Publishing Co., 1976.

Tukey, Harold Bradford, *Dwarfed Fruit Trees.* The Macmillan Co., 1964.

Welch, H. J., *Dwarf Conifers.* Faber and Faber, Ltd., London, 1966.

Wyman, Donald, *Dwarf Shrubs.* Macmillan Publishing Co., Inc., 1974.

Wyman, Donald, *Trees for American Gardens.* The Macmillan Co., 1965.

Wyman, Donald, *Wyman's Gardening Encyclopedia.* Macmillan Publishing Co., Inc., 1977.

Yoshimura, Yuji, and Halford, Giovanna M., *The Japanese Art of Miniature Trees and Landscapes.* Charles E. Tuttle Co., 1957.

Acknowledgments

The index for this book was prepared by Anita R. Beckerman. For their help in the preparation of this book, the editors wish to thank the following: The American Rose Society, Shreveport, La.; Ernesta D. and Frederic L. Ballard, Chestnut Hill, Pa.; Charles E. Bell Jr., Alexandria, Va.; Morris Berd, Media, Pa.; Lavia Berland, New York City; Dr. Willard P. Bitters, Dept. of Plant Sciences, University of California, Riverside, Calif.; Ellie Bogin, Long Beach, N.Y.; Sherry Boutard, Educational Director, Berkshire Garden Center, Inc., Stockbridge, Mass.; Pat Braun, Madderlake, New York City; William Brown, Coram, N.Y.; Burgess Seed and Plant Co., Galesburg, Mich.; Burpee Seed Co., Warminster, Pa.; Mr. and Mrs. Robert Choy, New York City; Mrs. John R. Clark, Villanova, Pa.; Dr. August DeHertogh, Dept. of Horticulture, North Carolina State University, Raleigh, N.C.; The Department of the Imperial Household, Tokyo, Japan; George Dodrill, McLean, Va.; Robert F. Doren, National Arboretum, Washington, D.C.; Robert Drechsler, Curator, National Bonsai Collection, National Arboretum, Washington, D.C.; Marnie Flook, Greenville, Del.; William Foster, Brunswick, Me.; Doris W. Froning, Kennett Square, Pa.; George W. Park Seed Co., Inc., Greenwood, S.C.; Charles Glass, Abbey Gardens Press, Santa Barbara, Calif.; Harold Greer, Greer Gardens, Eugene, Ore.; Marion Gyllenswan, Nanuet, N.Y.; George Hagar, American Orchid Society, Harvard Botanical Museum, Cambridge, Mass.; Dr. Ronald Hodges, Chief of Systematic Entomology Laboratory, U.S. Dept. of Agriculture, Beltsville, Md.; Mrs. John E. Hopkins, Wayne, Pa.; Frank K. Horwood, Abbey Garden, Carpinteria, Calif.; Professor Ryoji Iwasa, Chiba University, Chiba, Japan; Joyce Johnson, Newark, Del.; Jerome Kantor, Burpee Seeds, Warminster, Pa.; Michael J. Kartuz, Kartuz Greenhouses, Inc., Wilmington, Mass.; Doris and David S. Kaufman, Bluebell, Pa.; Russell Kirk, Temple Hills, Md.; Mrs. John S. Kistler, West Chester, Pa.; Joe and Marion Korninsky, West Chester, Pa.; Eleanor Laden, Philadelphia, Pa.; Dr. David Lellinger, Dept. of Botany, Museum of Natural History, Smithsonian Institution, Washington, D.C.; Dr. and Mrs. Maynard Lemrow, Farmingville, N.Y.; Lee Linnett, Clinton, Md.; Longwood Gardens, Kennett Square, Pa.; Lyndon Lyon, Dolgeville, N.Y.; Dr. Bruce McAlpin, Horticultural Specialist, New York Botanical Garden, Bronx, N.Y.; Yvonne McHarg, New York City; Rose Marie McMann, Wilmington, Del.; Dr. Robert O. Magie, Bradenton, Fla.; Don and Mary Marshall, San Mateo, Calif.; Anthony Mihalic, Wildwood Gardens, Chardon, Ohio; Moore Miniature Roses, Sequoia Nursery, Visalia, Calif.; John Y. Naka, Los Angeles, Calif.; Noweta Gardens, St. Charles, Minn.; Frank Okamura, Brooklyn Botanic Garden, Brooklyn, N.Y.; Ben Oki, Culver City, Calif.; Dr. Elwin R. Orton Jr., Cook College, Rutgers University, New Brunswick, N.J.; Margot Osborne, Assistant to the Curator, National Bonsai Collection, National Arboretum, Washington, D.C.; Jeannette Payton, Alexandria, Va.; James Pendleton, Good Earth Nursery, Burke, Va.; J. Liddon Pennock Jr., Meadowbrook Farm Greenhouse, Meadowbrook, Pa.; The Pennsylvania Horticultural Society, Philadelphia, Pa.; Richard Peterson, American Orchid Society, Harvard Botanical Museum, Cambridge, Mass.; Petoseed Co., Inc., Woodland, Calif.; Mrs. Andrew Porter, Villanova, Pa.; Clifton Pottberg, Baltimore, Md.; Kathryn Prichard, Hockessin, Del.; Sally Reath, Devon, Pa.; Albert and Lois Jean Rissman, Falls Church, Va.; Professor R. W. Robinson, Dept. of Seed and Vegetable Science, New York State Agricultural Experiment Station, Geneva, N.Y.; Chris Rosmini, Los Angeles, Calif.; Marjorie and William Rourke, Seattle, Wash.; Jean and Mark Salter, Chester, Pa.; Shohachi Sasaki, Japan Embassy, Washington, D.C.; Harmon Saville, Nor'East Miniature Roses, Inc., Rowley, Mass.; Stanley Schwartz, American Gloxinia and Gesneriad Society, Flushing, N.Y.; Peter Shalit, Seattle, Wash.; Stanwyn G. Shetler, Dept. of Botany, Smithsonian Institution, Washington, D.C.; Frances Shively, Director, Lee-Fendall House, Alexandria, Va.; R. H. Shumway, Seedsman, Rockford, Ill.; Dr. Laurence E. Skog, Dept. of Botany, Smithsonian Institution, Washington, D.C.; Gerald Smith, University of Georgia, Athens, Ga.; Joel W. Spingarn, Baldwin, N.Y.; Mr. and Mrs. Edward Starr, Bryn Mawr, Pa.; Jane Steffey, Horticultural Advisor, American Horticultural Society, Mount Vernon, Va.; Libby Stephenson, Wilmington, Del.; Dr. Allan K. Stoner, Research Horticulturalist, Science and Education Administration, Agricultural Research Vegetable Laboratory, U.S. Dept. of Agriculture, Beltsville, Md.; Jerald P. Stowell, Stockton, N.J.; A. Summerville, Summerville Nursery, Glassboro, N.J.; Rexford H. Talbert, Alexandria, Va.; Henry Wagner, La Habra, Calif.; Charles D. Webster, President, The Horticultural Society of New York, New York City; Father Peter Weigand, St. Anselm's Abbey School, Washington, D.C.; John Wheeler, The Japan Society, New York City; Renee White, Editor, *The Gloxinian,* Providence, R.I.; Ernest D. Williams, Mini-Roses, Dallas, Tex.; R. D. Williams, Plant Ecologist, Science and Education Administration, Water Quality Management Laboratory, U.S. Dept. of Agriculture, Durant, Okla.; Nona Wolfram, Pan American Seed Company, West Chicago, Ill.; Mildred Wood, Assistant to the Curator, National Bonsai Collection, National Arboretum, Washington, D.C.; Patrick Worley, Kartuz Greenhouses, Wilmington, Mass.; Dr. Hiroshi Yuasa, Tokyo Agricultural University, Tokyo, Japan.

Index

Numerals in italics indicate an illustration of the subject mentioned.